DECADE OF DISBELIEF

Decade of Disbelief

Chonka Bojack

Contents

1

Introduction: Trinitarian Virtue Ethics?

"We should seek not simply to promulgate a trinitarian theology, but to think and to live in trinitarian ways."
-David Cunningham, *These Three are One*
***

A friend once told me a joke that went something like this: The members of the Trinity, having created and sustained the universe for what seemed like an eternity, decided to take a vacation. Since they had been cooped up together for quite some time, they decided to plan their own separate vacations, so that they could each get some much-needed alone time. The Father said, "I think I'll go to Hawaii. I could use a little fun in the sun." The Son said, "I've had enough of Earth for awhile. Things didn't go so well for me when I was there last, and I'm not quite ready to go back. So I think I'll vacation on Mars." Finally, the Holy Spirit said, "Those sound like excellent vacation spots. As for myself, I think I'll take a little trip to the Vatican, since I've never been there."

Jabs at the Roman Catholic hierarchy aside, this joke also plays with some of our traditional understandings of the Trinity, turning trinitarian persons into human persons, who need vacations and get sick of one another. Indeed, for some people, the doctrine of the Trinity itself seems to be a joke (I certainly have gotten some strange looks when I tell people that I am working on trinitarian theology and virtue ethics!). For others, the Trinity might be a piece of irrelevant doctrine. When I told my mother, a lifelong Catholic, what I was working on, she asked, "How in the world does the Trinity relate to ethics?" I hope this project offers one way to answer that question.

This project emerges from the belief that our understanding of God affects how we understand ourselves and shapes our idea of the kinds of people we want to be. To make this point, I draw from contemporary interpretations of the Trinity to show how different perspectives on God can in turn give us different perspectives on and insights into the human person. I also propose virtues—good characteristics we want to embody—drawn from diverse understandings of the Trinity. Thus, this project brings together trinitarian theology and virtue ethics to bring more theological insight into how we understand ourselves and the kinds of people we want to become.

The timing is good for such a project. In the last fifty years, theologians have been working to recover the doctrine of the Trinity, and have created a flourishing field of trinitarian theology. During roughly the same time, Christian virtue ethicists have been working to incorporate more theology into their work, returning, for example, to scripture and the life of Jesus as the foundation for ethics. Despite renewals in both of these areas, not many thinkers have begun to draw out the implications of trinitarian theology for virtue ethics. For the most part, the theologians have done their work, and the ethicists have done theirs, with little overlap. Only a handful of thinkers have proposed a "trinitarian ethics"—an ethics in which the doctrine of the Trinity is the primary guide for determining what a moral person and behavior are. Even those who have proposed a trinitarian virtue ethics have used only one image of God as the source of their moral anthropologies. That is, despite the numerous theologians working on the Trinity, even those Christian ethicists who draw from the doctrine of the Trinity in their work have not taken full advantage of the wealth of trinitarian theology at their disposal. Thus, in this project, I argue for a trinitarian virtue ethics that employs *multiple* images of God. This approach will be beneficial in two major ways, as we will see. First, attending to diverse interpretations of the Trinity will preserve a sense of God's mystery and prevent one image of God from becoming hegemonic. Second, multiple images of God will offer a broader foundation for the anthropology of a trinitarian virtue ethics, opening more possibilities for understanding the human person and introducing new virtues.

Overview and Chapter Outline

In the following chapters, I examine the images of a triune God found in three contemporary theologians— John Zizioulas, Elizabeth Johnson, and Catherine Keller—in order to draw out implications for the moral anthropology of Christian virtue ethics. For each of these theologians, I give an overview and evaluation of their understandings of the Trinity. I examine how each draws from and employs scripture, tradition, reason, and experience in order to highlight the strengths and weaknesses of each theology. I then draw out the implications their images of God have for our understanding of the human person. From this foundation, I suggest specific virtues that are implied by each of their trinitarian images. In my discussion of the three theologians, I will be interested only in the images of the Trinity in their work and not with their larger constructive projects.

As I discuss the anthropologies, I introduce the feminist philosopher Luce Irigaray as an interlocutor. Several themes running through her work parallel those of the theologians I have chosen. Putting her in dialogue with each of their images of God will allow me to sharpen the definitions of the virtues implicit in those images.

In Chapter One, I briefly trace the resurgence of Christian virtue ethics. I show how virtue ethicists have begun to incorporate scripture and theology into their frameworks, as well as how more reflection on the Trinity is needed. I also overview the work of David

Cunningham, the first thinker to propose a trinitarian virtue ethics. I show how our projects are similar and how they are different.

In Chapter Two, I show the benefits of employing multiple interpretations of God and outline my basic methodological approach. I explain each of the four sources of theological knowledge—scripture, tradition, reason, and experience—and show how interpreting a theologian through his or her use of the four sources is helpful.

Chapters Three, Four, and Five are the central chapters of the dissertation. In each of these chapters, I examine the work of one theologian, examining his or her interpretation of the Trinity and the implications it has for how we understand ourselves and the kinds of virtues we want to practice.

In Chapter Three, I examine the theology of John Zizioulas, who offers an understanding of God as a communion of freely given love between unique and irreplaceable persons. Personhood is a key term for Zizioulas and, for him, suggests not individuality but communion. To say that a member of the Trinity is a person is to say that this member exists only in relation to the others; "to be and to be in relation become identical." Zizioulas also applies his understanding of divine persons to human persons. Personal uniqueness is established not against but in communion with others, and each person in this relational existence is unrepeatable and irreplaceable. Zizioulas' insistence on the absolute uniqueness of the person (both divine and human) leads him to recommend an "ethical apophaticism," which rejects any attempt to classify or categorize persons. I bring Irigaray's thoughts on difference and wonder into conversation with Zizioulas' theology and show that "wonder" emerges as the virtue implicit in his image of God.

In Chapter Four, I examine the theology of Elizabeth Johnson, who names in female terms—She Who Is—the God who "enlivens, suffers with, sustains, and enfolds the universe." She begins with Spirit-Sophia, who is God's personal engagement with and empowering presence in the world. Next is Jesus-Sophia, whose humiliating death on a cross overturns patriarchal understandings of masculinity. Finally, Mother-Sophia is the creative, life-giving force of all that exists. Johnson argues that the image of God as Mother opens up fresh ways of understanding God's compassionate, creative power. Johnson's symbol of God serves as a reminder that all of us—male and female—are equal in our dignity as creatures made in the image of God. I bring Irigaray's thoughts on cultivating female subjectivity into conversation with Johnson's theology and show that "self-esteem" emerges as the virtue implicit in her image of God.

In Chapter Five, I examine the theology of Catherine Keller, who reconsiders the doctrine of *creatio ex nihilo*, suggesting instead a creation out of the primal chaos, or *tehom*. In Keller's thought we find not an omnipotent God, but a God of interdependence. Keller names Tehom, the Depth of God and the matrix of possibility, as the first member of a Trinity of folds. This Depth is that which folds the world into God. The second member is the Difference of God, that which unfolds continually into the world. Thus, Depth as God enfolding all, and Difference as God unfolding into all. The third member of Keller's Trinity, the Spirit of God, is the relation of relations. The Spirit suggests not only a divine interdependency but also the interdependence of creator and creation, and of all creatures. Keller's theology is one "in which chaos replaces the nihil and in which flux, carefully mediated by forms of stability, permanence and order, remains primary." I bring Irigaray's thoughts on multiplicity and fluidity into conversation with Keller's theology and show that "open-endedness" emerges as the virtue implicit in her image of God.

In Chapter Six, I take the virtues I have named—wonder, self-esteem, and open-endedness—and apply them in three different ways. I first show how they can be employed as methodological virtues that will help determine more trinitarian images to use. I then show how the trinitarian virtues modify or shed light on some of the traditional cardinal virtues. Finally, I apply all three virtues to a final case study, showing how they can help churches become more fully welcoming of people with physical disabilities.

Significance

Engaging with multiple images of God offers resources for reflection not only on who God is but also on who we are and who we want to become. In examining the images of God in the work of Zizioulas, Johnson, and Keller, I show how different understandings of God can yield different insights into the human person. This project is significant in several ways. First, it will contribute to Christian virtue ethics a needed theological reflection on the human person by considering in depth the implications trinitarian theology has for our understanding of what it means to be human. Using trinitarian theology will help give Christian virtue ethics further insight into human relationality, and using multiple trinitarian images will encourage a moral anthropology that appreciates diversity and is able to include traditionally marginalized groups—the physically or mentally disabled, sexual minorities, etc.

Second, the project also contributes to trinitarian ethics, which has not yet explored how using multiple images of God might allow for more flexible interpretations of both God and the human person. Third, by drawing from the theologies of a Catholic, a Protestant, and an Orthodox Christian, the project will contribute to the ecumenical dialogue in Christian ethics. Fourth, by examining the work of two feminist theologians and engaging feminist philosophy, it will contribute to the field of women's studies in religion. Finally, and perhaps most importantly, by pulling out implications of trinitarian theology for virtue ethics, this project will help Christian pastors and laypeople apply their beliefs to their everyday lives. Because I have a background in catechesis and remain committed to the importance of good religious education, I hope this project will be accessible, interesting, and practical for everyday Christians.

When I first began my doctoral studies, I did not plan on employing virtue ethics as my primary ethical method. Virtue ethics seemed like the fashionable choice ("everybody's doing it!"), and, not wanting to follow the crowd, I resisted. Despite this initial resistance, I found virtue ethics intriguing and continued to explore it, yet for a time I still hesitated to claim it as my ethical framework. My resistance broke down one day when I realized that, in my real, day-to-day life, I was actually using virtue ethics. It struck me that many of the ways in which I make decisions—looking to role models, thinking of characteristics I'd like to embody, imagining the kind of person I wanted to become—were some of the key contributions of virtue ethics. So, while I was resisting virtue ethics academically, it turns out that I was already living it. Virtue ethics offers a practical approach to moral decision-making, takes a realistic picture of the contingencies of human life, and emphasizes the importance of the everyday, so it was, in the end, irresistible.

Just as certain experiences led me to adopt virtue ethics, so too did they spark an interest in trinitarian theology. In my college days, I assumed that the only way to refer to the Trinity was Father, Son, and Holy Spirit and that using the male pronoun for God exclusively was perfectly acceptable. Then one day, just as a little experiment, I used the female pronoun for God. I was amazed at the difference a simple switch—calling God "She"—made. Referring to God in the feminine, just once, made me think about God and myself completely differently. As I began to experiment with other names and images, as well as to read more theology, I became convinced that the words we use to name and describe God have a profound impact on how we understand ourselves, other people, God, and the world around us.

I hope that, in this dissertation, some of the practical implications of both virtue ethics and trinitarian theology will become clearer. Our understandings of God can have a major impact on how we understand ourselves. A trinitarian virtue ethics can help us make sense of different images of God and the ways in which they encourage certain virtues and compel us to become certain kinds of people.

James Gustafson notes that "religious symbols and theological concepts are used to interpret the significance of other persons, of events, and of the circumstances in which action is possible and required." The trinitarian symbols I examine and the virtues they suggest—wonder, self-esteem, and open-endedness—can thus help guide our attitudes and actions. Putting wonder into practice may help us learn to respect the mystery and humanness of the other; practicing self-esteem calls us to greatness and to make room for the greatness of others; practicing the virtue of open-endedness may enable us to unfold our differences and to let go of the ways in which we have used those differences oppressively. Trinitarian theology and virtue ethics can combine to help us navigate our assumptions, attitudes, decisions, and actions.

I try throughout this dissertation to emphasize both the mystery of God and the mystery of being human. Virtue ethics offers me a practical approach to moral decision-making that resists abstract and universal rules. Trinitarian theology offers me a number of unique interpretations of God that emphasize that our language for God always falls short and is never exhausted. In combination, these two fields offer a trinitarian virtue ethics that, I hope, emphasizes that there are always multiple perspectives on both God and human beings. Trinitarian virtue ethics encourages Christians to live flexibly within this multiplicity and to remember that our lives reflect the images of God in many different ways, which is something to be celebrated.

An Emerging Trinitarian Virtue Ethics: Where We Are Now

This project draws from two main areas: contemporary trinitarian theology and virtue ethics. The contributions of contemporary trinitarian theology will become evident in later chapters. In this chapter,

I overview the important contributions of virtue ethics to my project. I work within a virtue ethics framework throughout this dissertation, employing it both implicitly and explicitly, so it is important to note its central tenets. I begin with Thomas Aquinas's account of the virtues and then move into more contemporary accounts. I show how contemporary Christian virtue theorists have begun to draw more heavily from scripture and the life of Jesus in their work. From this, I suggest four common elements of a virtue ethic moral anthropology. I then overview the work of David Cunningham, the first thinker to propose a trinitarian virtue ethics.

Virtue Ethics

"To be an acorn is to have a taste for being an oak tree."
-Thomas Merton, *Thoughts in Solitude*

Joseph Kotva defines virtue ethics as that which "deals with the transition from who we are to who we could be." That is, virtue ethics aims to help us become a certain sort of person. A virtue ethic framework can be said to consist of three parts—a picture of who we are now, a picture of who we want to become, and a set of virtues that will help us get from one to the other. Because of this teleological focus, virtue ethics recognizes that as we grow physically and emotionally, we will also grow in virtue; becoming virtuous is necessarily a gradual process. Further, because acquiring virtues means practicing them, every moment of our lives is a chance to get better at being virtuous. As James Keenan puts it, virtue ethics sees "the ordinary as the terrain on which the moral life moves." Virtue ethics is, in short, a practical, person-centered approach to good living.

Much contemporary virtue ethics is rooted in the thought of St. Thomas Aquinas. Thomas argues that humans have three levels of natural inclinations: those that we share with all living things, namely the desire for self-preservation; those that we share with other animals, such as the desire to reproduce and raise children; and, finally, those that are distinctly human, which include our desire to know God and to live in community. Directing each of the inclinations is the first principle of practical reason: good is to be done and pursued, and evil avoided. This principle directs our inclinations to what is good for us.

In essence, for Thomas, reasoned reflection on our natural inclinations leads us to discover what is good for humans, and it is through virtue that we are able to discern how we ought to pursue these goods. As Jean Porter puts it, the virtues "stem from and are ineliminably shaped by the natural inclinations and needs of the human organism." The inclinations of humans can be expressed in ways that undermine our good. We can, for example, pursue goods, such as food or sex, immoderately or unjustly, so if the inclinations are "to function in such a way as to promote the agent's true good, they must be directed by appropriate dispositions toward action—and that is precisely what the virtues are." The virtues orient our inclinations toward our well being, so that we can pursue goods in a way that will make us happy. In other words, the virtues move us from who we are to who we want to become.

For Thomas, this idea of who we want to become—our human end or *telos*—involves a dual happiness; natural happiness is the happiness of this life and can be attained by our own efforts, and supernatural happiness is the happiness of the next life, which we attain only with God's help. We reach our end by means of the virtues. By performing certain kinds of actions, we develop habits, which in turn dispose us to keep acting in a certain way. Good habits are virtues and move us toward our *telos*, while bad habits are vices and move us away from it. Thomas argues that the virtues that direct us to our natural happiness are of two kinds—intellectual and moral. The intellectual virtues are divided into speculative (understanding, wisdom, science) and practical (art and prudence). The moral virtues (also called cardinal) are prudence, temperance, justice, and fortitude. The moral virtues train our appetites; prudence directs our reason, temperance governs the concupiscible appetites, fortitude governs the irascible appetites, and justice directs the will. We are born with the aptitude for these virtues, but it is only through consistent action that we actually acquire them; the acquisition of virtue is gradual and requires hard work.

Thomas further argues that the moral and practical intellectual virtues are interdependent. If we do not develop the intellectual virtues, especially prudence, our reason will apply itself poorly and will not be able to help us *choose* the fitting action. On the other hand, if we do not develop the moral virtues, we will not be able to *perform* the fitting action. Prudence is crucial here because it connects the intellectual and moral virtues and helps us apply principles of reason to specific circumstances.

The virtues that direct us to our supernatural end, Thomas suggests, are the three theological virtues of faith, hope, and charity. These virtues are infused in us as God's gift and are unattainable without God's grace. Moral virtues may also be infused, if the exercise of one is necessary for the exercise of a theological virtue. The infused moral virtues are put in the service of charity and direct us to supernatural happiness.

Thomas grounds his anthropology and virtue theory in natural law, offering universal inclinations and virtues that all humans ought to pursue, as well as the distinctly theological virtues of faith, hope, and charity that direct Christians to their supernatural end. Though his account is grounded theologically, it has tended to be interpreted philosophically, with his brief section on natural law receiving more attention than his sections on the virtues. In recent years, virtue theorists and other Christian ethicists, seeking to correct these more philosophical interpretations, have begun to emphasize Thomas' account of the virtuous life and have also turned to Scripture and the life of Jesus to demonstrate a more explicitly Christian virtue ethics.

Paul Wadell, for example, offers a fresh reading of Thomas' work, arguing that "the core of Thomistic ethics is not the natural law, but the virtues, and the virtues are best understood not as acts of reason, but as strategies of love whereby those devoted to God are transformed in God's goodness." Wadell critiques interpretations of Thomas that paint his work as too rationalistic, formal, or scholastic, arguing instead that it is practical and centered in love. He argues that Thomas understands every human action to be motivated by some desire and that the goal of the moral life is to cultivate our desires for good things and to weed out our desires for bad things. Thus for Thomas, the beginning of morality is not reason, Wadell argues, but the desire to respond to some good that has affected us. Our loves determine the kinds of persons we will be. What Thomas aims for in his moral theology, Wadell argues, "is nothing less than the remaking of our hearts" so that they are ever striving for friendship with God.

Wadell himself builds on Thomas' work, arguing that happiness—life with God—is the goal of the moral life. While Thomas focuses on the inclinations as the basis of his anthropology, Wadell has a more explicitly relational focus, arguing that "human beings are inherently and inescapably social beings who need to live in deep, intimate, enriching relationships with others." He focuses on one kind of relationship—friendship—arguing that all humans need friends and that all of our lives would be much poorer without them. Friendships are adventures, he claims, that help us discover our best selves and teach us how to care for others. Friendships are schools for the virtues of compassion and trust. Further, as a friendship develops, we find we can be honest and vulnerable, and we often find that our friends have insights into us that we ourselves do not have. All humans need relationships, Wadell argues, and, in particular, all humans need friendship—a mutual and gradual "unveiling of the self to another."

Friendship, then, has a definite affective component, which reinforces Wadell's argument that any moral theory must include a "synthesis of reason, emotions, perceptions, convictions, and intuitions." The desires and feelings in the body are an important aspect of the human person and must be given a place in any adequate moral anthropology. For Wadell, like Thomas, the goal of human life is friendship with God, but Wadell offers a more explicitly relational and holistic anthropology.

Wadell emphasizes the importance of freedom in pursuing this friendship with God and notes that freedom is not simply doing whatever we want. It is, rather, faithfulness to the good; "the greatness of freedom lies in the summons to use our freedom to share in and contribute to the creative and redemptive work of God." Exercising our freedom properly means remembering that we are created in the image of God, sustained by God's love, and called to do God's work on earth. Because we are naturally attracted to the good, he argues, the appropriate use of our freedom is to make choices that bring us closer to the good, that is, to God. The freest person is that one who "knows, loves, seeks, and serves the good."

Wadell also notes that friendships contribute to our freedom; "one of the great gifts of a good friendship is that each friend helps the other grow in freedom by helping them be more fully and authentically who they are called to be." Further, freedom is closely related to virtue:

A life of virtue is a life of freedom. An act of justice is not something other than freedom, but the way freedom is embodied and expressed in our relationships with others. Compassion is not something other than freedom, but how freedom is displayed in the face of suffering...We may be accustomed to think that the virtues limit freedom because freedom is the capacity to do anything...Freedom does not consist in endless possibilities of doing just anything; rather, freedom means faithfulness to the good.

For Wadell, freedom is not about license but about becoming who we really are.

Wadell also recognizes that we can easily misdirect our lives and forget who we are. He notes three truths about Christian identity: we are creatures, we are made in the image of God, and we are called to do the work of God. To sin is to forget that "our lives are not our own, they are God's gift to us...[and that] at every moment, God's love constitutes and sustains" us. When we sin, he argues, we mistakenly assert our independence from God and work against God's grace. Wadell's notion of sin emphasizes our creatureliness and stresses that we are constituted and sustained by God's love. He notes that because of sin, there is a gap between who we are now and who we want to become; filling this gap is the work of virtue. For Wadell, the virtuous Christian life "is an ongoing convalescence, a never-finished healing and rehabilitation through which we are reconnected to the good we initially rejected, the good we thought we could live without."

While Wadell's work continues in a Thomistic vein, highlighting the teleological nature of the Christian life, Joseph Kotva's work makes more explicit the relationship between Christian doctrine and virtue ethics, arguing that virtue theory is the best way to express many aspects of the Christian journey found both in classical doctrine and in scripture. First, Kotva looks at certain aspects of Christian theology to show how they correspond nicely with virtue theory. The doctrine of sanctification, for example, involves the development of character traits so that we grow more in conformity with Christ; it is teleological, with likeness to Christ as the ultimate goal. Kotva emphasizes that Christians depend on the help of grace in order to make the sanctifying transformation from who we are to who we could be (Christ-like). Virtue theory squares nicely with the Christian idea of sanctification because both emphasize character traits and development over time.

Kotva also draws comparisons between Christian anthropology and virtue ethics, showing how each emphasizes the importance of freedom in the moral life. According to Kotva, contemporary virtue theory falls somewhere between behaviorism and voluntarism on the issue of freedom; we are not completely determined by external factors, such as biology or culture, but neither are we absolutely free. Rather, he suggests, humans are contingent because we are bound to our bodies, historical situations, and beliefs, yet we retain the capacity to choose our actions within these contingencies. Because virtue ethics posits an active life in pursuit of virtue, a virtue ethic anthropology understands humans as "self-forming and determining agents" while also remaining realistic about our finitude. Christian anthropology enriches virtue theory here as well, suggesting that "human freedom unfolds only in response to God's Spirit" and that God's grace enables us to become who we are meant to be. Further, Kotva argues, both Christian theology and virtue ethics view the person in relationship and community; in neither case can the individual realize her potential in isolation.

In the area of Christology, Kotva argues that Jesus realized the full human potential and shows us "normative and paradigmatic humanity;" Christians know something of our *telos* because we have seen our end in Christ. Jesus shows us who we could be, and it is through a life of discipleship that we can become more like him. Virtue theory and Christology work well together because Jesus' life, death, and resurrection show what it really means to be human and demonstrate the traits or virtues that are constitutive of true humanity. Virtue theory calls us to become a certain kind of person; Christology shows us that person.

In addition to drawing comparisons between Christian doctrine and virtue theory, Kotva also explores virtue and scripture. He looks specifically at Matthew's Gospel and Paul's letters in an effort to begin sketching an interpretation of scripture through a virtue lens. He points to how Matthew uses role models and emphasizes character traits to show his readers what discipleship looks like. He also suggests that Matthew's Gospel highlights the importance of community in moral formation; Matthew's treatment of sin and reconciliation show that these are not simply personal matters, and the virtues of humility and forgiveness have social significance.

Kotva also points out similar tendencies in Paul that work well in a virtue framework. Paul holds himself up as a role model, calling people to imitate him as he imitates Christ. Kotva also points out Paul's lists of virtues, such as joy, peace, and kindness, and vices, such as arrogance, selfishness, and envy. In the areas of theology and scripture, Kotva is not exhaustive in showing their compatibility with virtue theory, but he makes some significant and convincing suggestions and opens the door for further exploration.

In addition to Kotva, William Spohn and James Keenan each look more carefully at the relationship between virtue ethics and Christianity, looking in particular at the role of Jesus. First, Spohn argues that "Jesus Christ is the paradigm for the Christian moral life" and that Christians, then, are to perform actions that are similar to Jesus' actions in the Gospels. This is what it means to be a disciple. For Spohn, a life of discipleship is not a literal imitation of Jesus' life, but rather a life that is faithful to the dispositions and actions of Jesus in new and different circumstances. Thus the Christian's life will reflect, in a creative and analogical way, Jesus' own life, which was "loving, faithful to God, compassionate to the suffering and oppressed, dedicated to justice, self-forgetful and God-centered, wise, courageous."

Spohn argues that the ethical system best equipped to help Christians in this kind of discipleship is virtue ethics. This is for three reasons. First, virtue ethics fits the narrative form of the New Testament and focuses on character. Because the Gospels are narratives, their central character, Jesus, becomes important; "the New Testament reveals who Jesus is and how he responds to God...His life gives the content to what it means that Yahweh is returning Israel to power: the blind see, the deaf hear, captives are released, the poor have the good news announced to them first." Virtue ethics will help Christians discern the qualities and dispositions of Jesus so that they can develop character traits that are similar to his.

Second, virtue ethics "attends to the deeper levels of moral existence which the teaching of Jesus addressed: the heart, the personal center of convictions, emotions, and commitments." Spohn notes that Jesus insisted that external obedience to laws was not enough; rather, especially in the Sermon on the Mount, Jesus counsels "dispositions of the heart" that operate at a deeper level. Jesus does not offer a detailed code of conduct, and neither does virtue ethics. Rather, Spohn argues, both focus on the "inner dynamics of disposition and motivation." Virtue ethics encourages certain practices that in turn nurture certain dispositions; because Jesus also focuses on inner dispositions, the language of virtue is a natural fit. Spohn notes the importance of spiritual practices in cultivating certain dispositions. Spiritual practices, such as regular prayer, train our affections, which in turn can evoke certain dispositions and direct our actions. He argues that gratitude and hope are the central affections for disciples of Jesus; "gratitude for unexpected gifts evokes a corresponding merciful love toward others and hope for reconciliation with those most distant from us through the work of justice."

The final link that Spohn suggests between virtue ethics and the life of Jesus is the importance of moral paradigms in each. Virtues are shaped by stories and exemplary figures that become paradigmatic; the Gospels are stories about Jesus, an exemplary figure who ought to be the paradigmatic figure on which Christians model themselves. In *What Are They Saying about Scripture and Ethics?* Spohn elaborates on the paradigmatic role of Jesus. He argues that Jesus is the concrete universal: "His *particular* story embodies a paradigmatic pattern which has *universal* moral applicability" (emphasis mine).

The experience of Jesus as concrete universal, Spohn suggests, guides three phases of our moral experience: perception, motivation, and identity. First, Jesus the concrete universal shapes our perception of the moral life by indicating *which features of our situation are morally significant.* Jesus ought to shape our vision of a particular situation—what does Jesus enable us to see? Jesus as concrete universal shapes our moral perception in such a way that makes us more sensitive to the plight of the poor and marginalized and allows us to envision ways "to heal the world, reconcile enemies, and transform oppression into justice."

The second way that Jesus functions as concrete universal is to show us *how* to act. The scriptural stories about Jesus become paradigms for *the kinds of actions* we ought to perform ourselves. Spohn notes that these paradigms function in two stages: first, they contain a discernable pattern, and second, there are procedures for applying the paradigms to new situations. Jesus' acts of compassion and forgiveness, for example, become guides for us as we discern the fitting action for our own circumstances. Finally, Jesus as concrete universal functions to show us *who* we are to become. The narratives of the Gospels show us the *kind of person* Jesus is, and as a particular person with universal significance, Jesus shows us the kind of people we ought to be.

In short, for Spohn, Jesus functions as the model we ought to follow and informs our moral lives at the levels of perception, motivation, and identity. The goal of the Christian moral life is "to follow Jesus, not to imitate him." The title of one of his books, *Go and Do Likewise,* indicates what it means to follow Jesus—to develop the dispositions and virtues that are presented in the New Testament and to apply these in creative ways to our own unique situations. For Spohn, Christian morality is about "catching the rhyme" between Jesus' life and ours; they will not be the same, but they will have common recognizable features that harmonize.

James Keenan also notes connections between scripture and virtue ethics. Like Spohn, Keenan argues that Jesus is the model for the Christian moral life. Drawing from an earlier theologian, Fritz Tillman, Keenan argues that Christian ethics "finds the source of its search for moral truth in the person of Jesus as the original image and the eventual goal for us." He notes that Jesus' life and message suggests three uniquely Christian virtues—mercy, a reconciling spirit, and hope. Jesus' Sermon on the Mount encourages these virtues, and they are embodied in the way he lived. Hope allows us to seek treasure in heaven, rather than on earth, to believe in God's providence, and to pray for anything we need. Further, since the kingdom of God is not yet fully realized, Christians live in hope, awaiting its full arrival. The virtue of a reconciling spirit enables Christians to be peacemakers and to love our enemies. Christians, having been reconciled to God in Christ, are in turn called to be "ambassadors of reconciliation," loving and forgiving one another along the way. Finally, mercy should guide all of our actions towards our neighbor. Keenan argues that mercy is the preeminent Christian virtue; "without mercy we do not have Christian ethics. Mercy is constitutive of the kingdom, and therefore, inasmuch as it pertains to the end, mercy precedes and shapes the content of Christianity." Keenan emphasizes God's own mercy, demonstrated in the parables of the lost coin, sheep, and son, and reminds us that Luke calls us to be merciful as our heavenly Father is merciful.

Keenan argues that these three virtues—mercy, hope, and a reconciling spirit—characterize the Christian life. They are drawn from scripture, especially from the accounts of Jesus' life, and thus are distinctly Christian in nature. Jesus embodied these virtues in his own life; they are "attributes of the one in whose image we are made and through whom we are saved." Christians seek these virtues to become more like Jesus, so as to participate in the coming kingdom of God.

Keenan's virtues of mercy and a reconciling spirit point to the relational nature of human beings. While many virtue ethicists stress our relationality, Keenan has given this aspect of moral anthropology particular attention. He notes that human beings are relational in three ways: we relate generally with all other people; we relate specifically with particular and special persons in our lives; and we relate uniquely with ourselves. To each of these modes of relating corresponds a virtue: in our general relationships with all others, we are called to justice; in our specific relationships, we are called to fidelity; and in our unique relationships with ourselves, we are called to self-care. Tying these three together is the virtue of prudence, which "determines what constitutes the just, faithful, and self-caring way of life for a particular individual." Keenan's relational anthropology emphasizes that we relate differently to different people, but the bottom line is that we are always relating—there is no one in the world to whom we are not somehow related.

Keenan argues that his relational anthropology is universal; "all persons in every culture are constituted by these three ways of being related." His cardinal virtues of justice, fidelity, self-care, and prudence are the minimum requirements for a virtuous person. All persons in all cultures must strive for these virtues of relationality, since they stem from basic anthropological facts, but each culture will add unique virtues on top of these to complete the picture of a truly virtuous person. As we have seen, Keenan suggests mercy, a reconciling spirit, and hope as distinctly Christian virtues that fill out a more specifically Christian way of relating. He defines mercy as the "willingness to enter into the chaos of another so as to respond to the other," which suggests that at every level of our relating, Christians will not be afraid of the messiness and vulnerability of human relationships; our pursuit of justice, fidelity, and self-care will be directed by a compassionate and merciful respect for all persons as made in the image of God.

By looking at the work of Wadell, Kotva, Spohn, and Keenan, we have seen how contemporary virtue theorists have supplemented Thomas' natural law virtue theory by drawing more intentionally from the Gospels and the life of Jesus. In addition to this thoughtful recovery of Thomas' virtue theory and the addition of virtues modeled on Jesus' example, such projects also give us insight into the ways in which Christian virtue ethicists understand the human person. In the next section, I examine four common elements of the anthropology of Christian virtue ethics.

A VIRTUE ETHIC ANTHROPOLOGY

In this section, I suggest common elements of a virtue ethic anthropology based on the above overview of virtue ethics. Because virtue ethics aims to help us transition from 'who we are' to 'who we could be,' an adequate virtue ethic must rest on a realistic, yet prophetic, anthropology ('who we are'); how we understand what it means to be human will influence our picture of human flourishing and our idea of the virtues that will help us get there.

First, we have seen that most Christian virtue theorists today argue that human beings are essentially relational; we become who we are only in relation to other people. Wadell emphasizes friendship; Kotva notes the communal nature of character formation; Keenan proposes virtues for each of the ways we are relational. Humans are not isolated individuals but are, rather, shaped, in minor or major ways, by those around us. In Richard Gula's words, "to think of a person without thinking of that person in relationship is to miss what it means to be a person." Christian virtue theorists resist individualistic anthropologies, asserting instead that "we are essentially relational, that is, open to the world, to others, and to God" and that all humans need relationships in order to fully flourish.

The second point of emphasis in a virtue ethic anthropology is embodiment. Contemporary Christian virtue theorists aim to give the body—with its desires, affections, and limitations—its rightful place in a holistic anthropology. It is, after all, only through our bodies that we can experience ourselves, others, and God; we can only learn to love and to be loved in and through our bodies. Contemporary Christian virtue theorists, such as Spohn, also emphasize the important part our affections play in our lives; without our emotions, we could not learn empathy, could not feel regret, or gratitude, or love, all of which are morally important. Christian virtue ethicists thus reject the split between reason and emotion, arguing instead that the two mutually influence and condition one another.

An increased attention to our embodiment is evident in the focus, as in Kotva, on the particular and historical nature of the individual, showing that when and where we are embodied makes us vulnerable to certain historical and cultural contingencies. We have also seen an increase in virtues that have a distinct affective component—such as compassion, mercy, and forgiveness—which reinforce the importance of embodiment and emotion in virtue ethics. Many of these virtues are drawn from the life of Jesus.

Richard Gula notes that the mystery of the incarnation is a profound affirmation of the body; "It proclaims that God comes to us in and through bodily form and that we, in turn, must relate to others, the world, and God in and through our bodiliness." In short, Christian virtue theorists recognize the dubious place the body has held throughout much of the Christian tradition and aim to counter this trend by emphasizing both the body's goodness and its importance in our moral lives.

A third component Christian virtue ethicists often include in their anthropologies is sinfulness. Though Christians believe that we are created in God's image, fashioned out of love and called to fellowship and respectful relationships with one another, we also acknowledge that we can often fall very short of this. We can be petty, mean, disrespectful, violent—towards God, others, or ourselves. Human relationality is both the source of great good and of great harm; most Christian virtue ethicists will define sin as broken relationship or as a failure to recognize our interconnectedness. Keenan, for example, will define sin as "not bothering to love;" Spohn will define it as self-absorption; and Kotva argues that through sin we are "imprisoned by self-centeredness." For these virtue theorists, sin is an abuse or misuse of our relationality.

Of course, being in relationship can be a tricky thing. "The downside of a relational identity," as Spohn puts it wryly, "is that we are related to people we do not want to be related to." Our own sinfulness, and that of others, sometimes makes our relationality seem more of a burden than a gift; certain relationships can cause deep pain or anger that may make us want to withdraw into ourselves. Sin turns us in on ourselves, causing us to be selfish and to forget the importance of our relationships with others.

Christian virtue theorists do not idealize our relationality and recognize that we do not always act like the kinds of people we want to be. In short, Christian virtue theorists recognize the reality of sin and the ways in which we can selfishly turn away from others or from God. Attention to sin acknowledges the messiness and fragility of human life and relationships.

A fourth and final general characteristic in a virtue ethic anthropology is freedom. In order to actively pursue the virtues, we need the freedom to be able to make choices. Kotva argues that though we are not absolutely free, neither are we entirely constrained by forces beyond our control. Wadell emphasizes freedom as the ability to pursue the good. Gula speaks of our freedom in terms of self-transcendence; we have the ability to reach out of ourselves and to move toward others and to God. We are not entirely constrained by social constructions, nor does God determine the path of our lives for us. Rather, God allows us the freedom to choose our own way. In short, Christian virtue theorists recognize that, although we are finite and partially socially constructed, we also have the power of agency. We are free to choose the good or to turn away from it.

While Christian virtue theorists have different points of anthropological emphasis, we can look to these four factors—relationality, embodiment, sinfulness, and freedom—as central components of a virtue ethic anthropology. This anthropology considers the whole person—reason, body, affections—situated in certain social and historical circumstances. Many of the contemporary insights into anthropology and the virtues result from the increased attention virtue ethicists have given to scripture and the life of Jesus.

Throughout this project, I remain indebted to these and other virtue theorists. By attending in more depth to trinitarian theology, I hope to continue the conversation they have begun between Christian theology and virtue ethics and to offer further insights into Christian anthropology and virtues. In the next section, I briefly overview the work of David Cunningham, who has begun this conversation between the doctrine of the Trinity and virtue ethics.

David Cunningham's Trinitarian Ethics

***

"The doctrine of the Trinity is a challenge to the modern cult of the individual; it teaches us to think in terms of complex webs of mutuality and participation. The practice of trinitarian theology thus calls us into newness of life—a life that bears a very different shape from what we have come to regard as 'ordinary' existence."

-David Cunningham, *These Three are One*

Only a handful of thinkers have proposed a trinitarian ethics—an ethics in which the doctrine of the Trinity guides and shapes the whole ethical framework. The most prominent of these, and the only one to focus on the Trinity and virtue ethics in particular, is David Cunningham. Cunningham, in *These Three are One*, offers his constructive proposal for a trinitarian virtue ethics. The book is divided into three parts: the first part traces the historical development of the doctrine of the Trinity and gives Cunningham's interpretation of that doctrine; the second part draws from Cunningham's interpretation of the Trinity to propose three trinitarian virtues—participation, polyphony, and particularity; and the final section offers three trinitarian practices—peacemaking, pluralizing, and persuading—that the virtues encourage. Below I focus on his elaboration of the trinitarian virtues.

Cunningham's virtues are drawn from his interpretation of the Trinity; they are qualities of God that humans can and ought to embody. In fact, the virtues are the "three key elements of God's triune character." The first virtue, polyphony, has to do with multiplicity. Drawing an analogy from music, Cunningham argues that a number of melodies can combine to make a pleasing sound. Some people may fear that the "only alternative to a single melody line is a pure cacophony of disjoint sounds," but he disagrees. The virtue of polyphony works to include different voices by playing more than one note at a time, ensuring that no one note is so dominant that it drowns out the others. For Cunningham, the virtue of polyphony means making music together out of our differences. This is drawn from his polyphonic understanding of the Trinity, "in which *difference* provides an alternative to a monolithic homogeneity, yet without becoming a source of exclusion."

Cunningham's second trinitarian virtue, participation, deals with relationality. He notes that the members of the Trinity are not simply relational, but that they are mutually indwelling and indwelt. Though their polyphony stresses their differences, their participation in one another means that their very uniqueness is shaped and informed by the others; "the Three *participate* in one another in a profound way, undermining any attempt to understand them independently of one another."

Cunningham suggests that humans are called to the same kind of participation. He prefers to call this virtue "participation" rather than "relationality" because "relationality" is not specific enough; relationships, as we saw in the last section, are not necessarily good in themselves because they can be insincere or abusive. The virtue of participation calls to mind the mutual indwelling of the Trinity and "means that we must be willing to allow others to shape our lives in profound and fundamental ways." Practicing this virtue in our contemporary context, he notes, is a difficult task because "our culture is profoundly antitrinitarian." We are taught to be independent and self-sufficient, rather than to recognize and appreciate that our lives are intertwined with those of others and that they shape us in significant ways. For Cunningham, the virtue of participation is perhaps the most difficult trinitarian virtue for us to practice.

Cunningham's third virtue, particularity, has to do with uniqueness. Each member of the Trinity, though profoundly shaped by the others, is nonetheless unique and distinct. Cunningham notes that the names we give to the Trinity emphasize their distinctness; the Father is the Father, not the Son or the Holy Spirit. Likewise, the virtue of particularity, for humans, means that we are ourselves and not anyone else. This does not, however, mean that we are isolated individuals. For Cunningham, our relationships with others—our participation—shape our unique identities. He uses a riverbed as an analogy. A riverbed has its own unique shape, form, and composition, but this particularity is only shaped, formed, and composed through an encounter with others—the water of the river, dirt, and other elements carried along with the river. We, too, are like this sedimented riverbed; our particularity and uniqueness is only established through our interactions with others. In Cunningham's words, "our particular existence is something we have *as a result* of our participation in a diverse world, not 'in spite of' that participation."

Cunningham's three virtues—polyphony, participation, and particularity—are drawn from his understanding of the Trinity as a melody of diversity, with members mutually indwelling and indwelt, deeply shaped by one another into unique and particular entities. Cunningham's work is the first to make explicit and sustained connections between the doctrine of the Trinity and virtue ethics. In some ways, our projects are very similar, yet they are also different.

My own project is motivated by the same basic belief as Cunningham's: "the way we understand God affects the way we understand our relation to God and our relation to one another; thus, the articulation of a doctrine of the Trinity has concrete ethical implications." Both of our projects attempt to show how the doctrine of the Trinity can shape our understanding of the Christian moral life. We both choose virtue ethics as our ethical framework and note characteristics of God that humans can and ought to embody as well. Finally, we both remain open to the possibility of error or new information. Cunningham emphasizes the fallibility of our discourse and questions "our desire to find absolute, final, risk-free solutions to the theological problems that we face." In my own way, I also emphasize the shortcomings of our language for God, the incompleteness of any given interpretation of the Trinity, and the ultimate unknowability of God. Neither my project nor Cunningham's offers definitive answers but rather seeks to offer one perspective on the ways in which the mystery of the Trinity can shape human life.

There is one primary difference between Cunningham's work and my project. He offers three virtues that stem from one interpretation of the Trinity. His interpretation of the Trinity draws from the historical development of the doctrine, though he adds his own spin. Rather than employing the traditional names, for example, he prefers to refer to the members of the Trinity as Source, Wellspring, and Living Water. Further, he eschews the language of "person" when referring to the trinitarian members. In fact, he refuses to say what they are at all, instead referring simply to "the Three." From his interpretation of the Trinity, he offers his virtues of polyphony, participation, and particularity as qualities that God has that humans can and should also embody.

Whereas Cunningham employs one interpretation of the Trinity to offer a number of virtues and practices, I take an almost opposite approach, employing multiple interpretations of the Trinity and offering only one virtue from each. In some ways, our approaches are complementary; Cunningham's approach offers an in-depth examination of one trinitarian image, while mine offers reflection on multiple images. My project could also be seen as an extension of Cunningham's. In *These Three are One,* he argues that future work on the Trinity should "testify to its profound significance for the shape of human life." By employing multiple interpretations of the Trinity and exploring their implications for virtue ethics, I hope to contribute to this testimony.

In short, Cunningham's work begins a needed conversation between trinitarian theology and virtue ethics; my project continues that conversation. In this chapter, we have seen the basic framework of virtue ethics, as well as how contemporary Christian virtue theorists have incorporated scripture and the life of Jesus into their work. We saw how this attention to the life of Jesus contributes in part to an increased emphasis on relationships, embodiment, freedom, and the reality of sin. We also saw how David Cunningham's work begins to bring together trinitarian theology and virtue ethics, thus continuing to conversation between theology and ethics. In the next chapter, I show why employing *multiple* images of God in a trinitarian virtue ethics is good for both God and humans. I also explain the four sources of theological knowledge—scripture, tradition, reason, and experience—and show how reading a theologian through his or her use of these sources can give us insight into the strengths and weaknesses of his or her particular interpretation of the Trinity.

2

The More the Merrier

"**D**o I contradict myself?
Very well then I contradict myself,
(I am large, I contain multitudes.)"
 -Walt Whitman, *Song of Myself*

As we saw in the last chapter, while Christian virtue theorists have done well to reflect on how the life of Jesus might affect virtue ethics, they have given the Trinity only a cursory glance. Those working in the small field of trinitarian ethics, such as David Cunningham, have reflected more deeply on the implications of trinitarian theology for our moral lives. Yet even these trinitarian ethicists have not fully explored the depth of trinitarian theology. In the last one hundred years, trinitarian theology has blossomed, but ethicists of all stripes have been slow to fully incorporate the new developments into their work. It is the aim of this dissertation to show that using a number of these interpretations of the Trinity in ethical reflection can offer new insights into the human person and the kinds of virtues we want to pursue. In chapters three, four, and five, I explore some of these trinitarian theologies, asking what they might mean for how we understand who we are, the kinds of people we want to become, and the kinds of characteristics we would like to embody. In the final chapter, I further consider the advantages of employing multiple images of God in our ethical reflection.

Before all this, however, some methodological considerations are in order. Why should we use multiple interpretations of the Trinity? What are the advantages of doing so? How do we know which images to use? Will using a number of interpretations be too chaotic? In the present chapter, I both offer some preliminary thoughts on the advantages of employing multiple images of God in ethical reflection and offer a way to navigate and critique these images. The chapter is divided into two parts: first, I reflect on the metaphorical nature of theological language to show how using multiple interpretations of the Trinity both preserves a sense of God's mystery and offers more ways to understand what it means to be human. Second, I offer the four traditional sources of theological knowledge (scripture, tradition, reason, and experience) as a method of gauging the suitability of particular interpretations of God.

Inexhaustible Mystery: Why Using Multiple Images is Good for God and Humans

The resurgence of trinitarian theology in the 20th century offered many new perspectives on and interpretations of the doctrine of the Trinity. While this new diversity has troubled some theologians who have argued that we must continue to use only the traditional language and formulation, other theologians have argued that, "rather than a situation to be bemoaned, the never-ending character of theology that drives its practitioners back to the drawing board is actually a great strength of the discipline." In this section, I hope to show that the variety of trinitarian images that have surfaced in the past one hundred years serve both to preserve a sense of God's mystery and offer more ways of understanding the human person, thus strengthening not only theology but also theological anthropology.

First, exploring new names for and understandings of God acknowledges God's mystery. In our "naming towards God," as Elizabeth Johnson puts it, we can never fully describe God or find the perfect language because God is ultimately beyond all description and language. The Trinity is one of the great mysteries of the Christian faith. In everyday terms, when we think of the word "mystery," we might think about a sleuth like Sherlock Holmes; detectives grab their magnifying glasses and their pipes, gather clues, and solve the mystery. And when we read mystery novels, part of the fun is to try to figure it out—solve the mystery—before the characters do. In short, in our everyday language, a mystery is something that can be solved. Theological mysteries, however, remain unsolved. With this kind of mystery, there is always something more to say, always another clue to find. Theologically speaking, a mystery is something that, no matter how hard we try to explain it, or how many ways we try to describe it, we still do not do it justice. Thus, the multitude of interpretations of the Trinity respects the mystery of it; we could go on talking about it forever and still not exhaust the mystery. For theological detectives, the game is always afoot, and theological mysteries are ultimately unsolvable: "When we think we've finally *got* it, haven't we already lost it?"

Thus, if we subscribe to only one interpretation of the Trinity, we close down other perspectives and resist entering the mystery. Sallie McFague has offered an understanding of theology as *heuristics* that is intentional about including many images of God. As she explains it, heuristic theology is one that is constantly seeking, imagines possibilities, and dares to think differently about God. This way of doing theology, she argues, is more experimental, imagistic, and pluralistic than other ways. Heuristic or metaphorical theology remains always aware of God's mystery and the limitations of human language; it supports the notion that "our concept of God is precisely that—*our concept* of God—and not God."

Because, as McFague notes, the concept of God is more than we can understand or describe, we employ metaphors for God that help us to describe our experiences of God. George Lakoff and other cognitive linguists have argued that metaphors do not just happen at the level of language, but at the level of thought and reason; the locus of metaphor is "in the way we conceptualize one mental domain in terms of another." For example, when we say "love is a journey," the metaphor is not the words themselves but rather the set of conceptual correspondences the words evoke. When we think of what a journey entails—a destination, a vehicle, bumps along the way—these characteristics of a journey map over to our understanding of love: the destination becomes sharing common life goals, the vehicle becomes the relationship, and the bumpy road becomes potential problems or conflicts in the relationship. If a vehicle breaks down during a journey, we can try to fix it and get it going again, we can remain in the vehicle and give up on reaching the destination, or we can abandon the vehicle. The same is true of love: we can try to work out our problems, stay in a relationship even though it is broken, or abandon the relationship altogether.

What the example of "love is a journey" shows us is that metaphors work at a conceptual level and map ideas from a more concrete domain (journey) onto a more abstract domain (love). What we can say concretely about one domain, what Lakoff calls the source domain, we can also say metaphorically about the more abstract, or target, domain.

Our metaphors for God work in the same way. Take the metaphor, "God is Father:" what does the concrete domain of "Father" tell us about the abstract domain of "God?" What do Fathers do? They beget children; they protect their children; they punish their children when they misbehave. Thus, if God is Father, humans are metaphorically God's children. God created us; God protects us; God punishes us when we sin. Metaphors can also have unintended consequences. Because the source domain (Father) draws on everyday experience, our experience of that domain colors our interpretation of the metaphor. Thus, it is also possible to say of fathers: Fathers are abusive; they are unreliable; they abandon their children, etc. These understandings of fathers become problematic when we map them onto the domain of "God;" most people do not want to think of God as unreliable or abusive. Metaphorical language thus has its potential pitfalls because metaphors are not precise and are open to interpretation. The unintended consequences of metaphors are called entailments. As we explore metaphors for God, it is important to keep in mind any negative entailments they might have. Because all metaphors have these entailments, no one metaphor will ever be entirely satisfactory by itself.

Cognitive linguist Eve Sweetser and biblical scholar Mary Therese DesCamp have worked together to suggest some implications of our metaphorical language for God. I highlight three of those implications below. First, Sweetser and DesCamp argue that different metaphors change the understanding of the relationship between God and humans. For example, the perceived relationship between God and humans will be different if we use the metaphor "God is friend" instead of "God is father." Thus, the authors argue, "metaphors actually constitute a relationship with God in crucial ways." The second implication of metaphorical language for God (and all metaphorical language) is that metaphors highlight some aspects of reality and not others. One metaphor cannot capture the full reality of God or all aspects of human experience of God. The metaphor of father, then, might do a good job of capturing some aspects of God, such as nurturing and protection, but it does not capture everything. The metaphor of friend might better capture God's trustworthiness, for example. Because individual metaphors do not capture the full reality of God, it thus becomes important to employ more than one to be able to understand and appreciate the many aspects of God. Using new and multiple metaphors, the authors note, "means new entailments, new things highlighted, new things hidden, new cognitive structures with which one can reason about God, new implications about God and humans." The final point that DesCamp and Sweetser make is that culture plays a large role in our metaphors. That is, the metaphors we use are not simply personal but have been shaped by a community. Further, we cannot escape the metaphors a particular community or culture uses;

"the mere existence of a particular common metaphor in one's culture means that the metaphor affects a person whether he or she likes it or not, or personally believes it or not." Awareness of the common metaphors for God—such as Father or King—will enable us to examine the ways in which the Christian community has been shaped by these metaphors.

Many theologians, too, have noted implications of our metaphorical God-language. Feminist theologians in particular have been vocal about employing new and varied metaphors for God. Elizabeth Johnson, for instance, argues that using just one metaphor for God tends to be oppressive and idolatrous; this absolutizes one metaphor and "obscures the height and depth and length and breadth of divine mystery." In the past 40 years, feminist theologians have offered a diverse array of interpretations that reflect various experiences and understandings of God. In the following few pages, I highlight several of these interpretations, grouped in three sections: first, feminist theologians dealing with the metaphor of father; second, feminist theologians focusing on the language of God in worship; third, feminist theologians who have interpreted the Trinity from particular theological perspectives. The theologians I mention in the following pages are not meant to give an exhaustive account of feminist theology. The aim, rather, is to show some of the ways in which theologians have challenged certain metaphors for God and have offered new perspectives on this ultimate mystery.

First, the conversation between early feminist theologians centers around the metaphor of God the Father. Critiquing Christian theology from a radical feminist perspective, Mary Daly argues that theological systems have been developed under the conditions of patriarchy and serve the ends of a sexist society. The symbol of God the Father reinforces patriarchy, preventing women from understanding themselves as being in the image of God and suggesting that their subordination to men is divinely ordained. Daly argues for a "castrating of language" in order to free human becoming from oppressive powers and to reestablish women's right to name God for themselves. When women take steps to move out of patriarchal space and language, she concludes, they are creatively participating in God the Verb, the "form-destroying, form-creating, transforming power that makes all things new." Daly rejects the metaphor of Father.

Picking up on Daly's critique, Sallie McFague suggests that the metaphor of God the Father has become literalized and hegemonic. Because all of our words for God, she argues, are "metaphors of experiences of relating to God," we are free to use many models but should be careful not to absolutize any one of them. Writing as a reformer within the Christian tradition, McFague does not reject the metaphor of God the Father, nor does she think the roots of Christianity are patriarchal; for her, unlike Daly, liberation can be found within a Christian paradigm, if we are able to keep our metaphors metaphorical.

We also find Rosemary Radford Ruether working as a feminist reformer within the Christian tradition. Citing "the promotion of the full humanity of women" as her guiding principle, Ruether offers a feminist systematic theology that opens possibilities for women's liberation within Christian thought. Ruether notes that masculine metaphors for God have reinforced a gender hierarchy; women relate to men as men relate to God. She sees a need to name God using both male and female metaphors while also moving beyond these to more gender-neutral metaphors, such as liberator and redeemer.

Finally, we come to Diane Tennis who warns us, "Do not abandon God the Father." While not clinging exclusively to this metaphor and arguing for the need to have female symbols for God as well, Tennis nonetheless sees great value in the image of God the Father. She does note problems with the traditional understanding of the Father as powerful, dominant, and distant, and she critiques this understanding by pointing to instances in scripture in which God is portrayed as present, available, tender, and reliable. Writing out of the experience of having been abandoned by her own father, Tennis argues that we must uphold these examples of a compassionate, gentle, and reliable

Father God as models for human fathers. Working not only within the Christian paradigm but also within the dominant Father model, Tennis offers her image of God the Father as an internal critique of patriarchy and as a challenge to human fathers.

These four early discussions of the language of God the Father challenged the male-dominated tradition and called for women's experience to be taken into account. Each of these theologians reminds readers of the metaphorical nature of language. While each judges differently the appropriateness of the metaphor of Father, they all make clear the need to de-literalize our language about God.

Second, feminist theologians have also been critical of the language for God used in worship. Ruth Duck, for example, has addressed the traditional baptismal formula ("I baptize you in the name of the Father, and of the Son, and of the Holy Spirit"). Echoing earlier concerns about the literalization of metaphors, Duck argues that the standard formula "epitomizes the contradiction between the church's offer of new life through Jesus Christ and its use of language reflecting patriarchal social systems." She insists that a revision of the formula is urgently needed and that alternatives should be judged in terms of their naming of God, their liturgical appeal, their resonance with scripture, and their ability to cross denominational lines. Duck offers her own revised formula, which is dialogical and gender-neutral:

Do you believe in God, the Source, the fountain of life?
I believe.
Do you believe in Christ, the offspring of God embodied in Jesus of Nazareth and in the church?
I believe.
Do you believe in the liberating Spirit of God, the wellspring of new life?
I believe.

Duck argues that her trinitarian baptismal formula is a fresh and evocative statement of Christian faith that moves beyond the patriarchal limitations of the traditional formula and satisfies the criteria she has set forth.

Gail Ramshaw and Patricia Wilson-Kastner also bring a feminist eye to the trinitarian language of Christian worship. Ramshaw notes that the Father-Son-Holy Spirit model "is on life-support" because of historical baggage with male language. She urges the Christian community to move toward using gender-inclusive terms in the search for "better, truer, clearer, more faithful language about the God it knows as triune." Wilson-Kastner, also guided by pastoral concerns, argues first, that the Trinity is central to Christian faith and worship and second, that our language for God should be gender-inclusive. Echoing earlier arguments about the metaphorical nature of language, Wilson-Kastner argues that our words for God should include "a constellation of metaphors that includes yet goes beyond" the traditional Father-Son-Holy Spirit language. She offers suggestions for preaching and liturgical resources that will help free our imaginations to praise God in many ways and with many names.

Finally, feminist theologians have approached the Trinity from a variety of theological perspectives and have shown how our interpretations of God are shaped by different kinds of experiences. Marjorie Suchocki, for example, offers a reformulation of trinitarian language from the perspective of process theology, in which existence is understood as a series of relational "instances of becoming." She argues that the metaphors of Father, Son, and Spirit have historically relative meaning and are no longer adequate for expressing our current experience of the triune God. Originally, she argues, the trinitarian language suggested wisdom and inclusivity, whereas today it confronts us with an oppressive maleness. In order to be true to our own experience of God as well as to the meaning of the original words, we find that we must use different language. Suchocki offers a new trinitarian formulation as power (Father), presence (Son), and wisdom (Spirit). For her, the problem is not the original revelation of God in terms of Father, Son, and Holy Spirit but rather that our contemporary historical situation obscures the real meaning of these metaphors, so that we find ourselves "in the topsy-turvy position of using the same words equivocally, conveying a meaning far removed from the revelation in Christ of God for us." Both the original formulation and hers, then, express our experience of a God for us, in whose goodness, wisdom, and nearness we can hope, but in different, historically relative terms.

Karen Baker-Fletcher has redefined the Trinity from a womanist perspective, emphasizing "God's courageous, gracious, relational, Trinitarian response to the unnecessary violence that affects the entire earth." Baker-Fletcher uses the metaphor of a dance to describe the Trinity as dynamic, integrative, and relational, participating in one common work of love, creativity, and justice. She further argues that because our experience of God transcends gender, our language for God should not be gendered. She offers the formulation of parent, wisdom or word, and breath or spirit as more appropriate God language, since these terms suggest God's nature as provident, nurturing, empowering, comforting, unifying, and present in ways that move us beyond gender. Further, this language and these images reflect our experience of God's grace and compassionate presence in a broken and violent world, calling us to join with God in a creative, courageous response.

Finally, Marcella Althaus-Reid, urging us to "keep decency at bay," offers some mischievous trinitarian thoughts from the perspective of queer theory and liberation theology. Althaus-Reid does her theology from the margins of sexual deviance and economic exclusion, seeking to rediscover God outside of the dominant heterosexual ideology of Christian theology and history. Beginning with the experiences of Queer, libertine bodies, she argues for a similar "queering of the Trinity;" Althaus-Reid's God is polyamorous, immoderate, and omnisexual, imbued with a sense of "twisted transcendence." This wild, passionate, indeterminate Trinity destabilizes heterosexual constructions of sexuality, thereby liberating both theology and people from normalizing discourses. One of her primary metaphors is God as orgy.

Just in these few examples, we have seen many different metaphors for God, and there are many more examples that I could have given. Each of the examples offers a distinct perspective on God and draws from different aspects of human experience and the Christian tradition. As we have seen, employing a number of metaphors for God acknowledges this diversity of experiences of and perspectives on who God is, preventing one image from becoming stale and hegemonic. Although a multitude of metaphors can lead to tensions between interpretations of God, ultimately only a diversity of images truly acknowledges God's mystery and the variety of ways in which God can be experienced:

Theologians' continuing struggle with and debate about the formulation of the doctrine is but another way of responding to the call of the church to both understand and express the faith revealed in the Bible and tradition for each new generation. This continuing dialogue among various, at times diverse, even contrasting voices is the fertile soil out of which real spiritual fruit grows.

MULTIPLE IMAGES OF GOD AND THEOLOGICAL ANTHROPOLOGY

Just as "there is always more to divine Mystery than human beings can nail down," so too is there more than one interpretation of what it means to be human. Employing a number of images of God not only preserves a sense of God's mystery but can also offer more perspectives on the human person; trinitarian theology tells us not only about God but also about ourselves. Theological anthropology is the area of theology that reflects on what it means to be a human being in relationship to God. Theological anthropology seeks to answer these questions (among others): What characteristics are uniquely or normatively human? What does it mean to be created in the image of God? Is there a universal human nature? If so, what is it? How does theological reflection on creation, fall, incarnation, and redemption affect how we understand what it means to be human? Our metaphors for and interpretations of God can play a major role in how we understand ourselves as human beings. In this section, I focus on the ways in which different understandings of God imply different kinds of relationships between God and humans. How we understand our relationship with God in turn affects our understanding of ourselves. This section is relatively brief; I explore in more depth the effects our images of God can have on our self-understandings in the following chapters.

First, as I mentioned in the previous section, Sweetser and DesCamp note that our metaphors for God affect how we understand our relationship with God; the more metaphors we use, the more perspectives we get on our relationship with God. If, for example, we use the common metaphor "God is Father," we can discover a certain understanding of the relationship between humans and God. Based on the scriptural use of the metaphor of father, Sweetser and DesCamp map out the implications in the chart below:

METAPHOR: GOD IS FATHER

Source domain: Father	Target domain: God
Father is agentive human male	God is conscious, agentive

Has mutual, asymmetric relationship with children	Has mutual, asymmetric relationship with all humans
Has physical control and authority over children; can discipline and punish	Can reward or punish all humans
Provides physical sustenance, nurture, and protection of children	Provides physical sustenance, nurture, and protection through Jesus and community
Provides inheritance within social structures	Provides inheritance to all who obey and honor
Love for children can be extravagant and undeserved	Love for humanity is extravagant and undeserved

Children have responsibility to obey and honor	All humans have responsibility to obey and honor

From this, we can infer a certain kind of relationship between God and humans: if God is Father, then humans are God's children and relate to God in ways that children relate to fathers. Thus, the relationship is asymmetric, with the father having control and authority over the children, the children are dependent on the father for sustenance and protection, and the children are subjects of the father's extravagant love.

As we saw earlier, a single metaphor, although helpful, cannot capture the full reality of God. If we use only the metaphor of God as father, it not only limits our understanding of God but also limits our understanding of our relationship to God, and thus also our understanding of ourselves. Using multiple metaphors enables us to envision our relationship to God in numerous ways. If we also use the metaphors of friend, lover, mother, sister, etc, we begin to imagine new ways of relating to God. For example, consider the brief chart below of the metaphor "God is friend."

Metaphor: God is Friend

Source domain (Friend)	Target domain (God)

Friends can be male or female	God can be understood in masculine or feminine terms
A friend is trustworthy and supportive	God can be trusted
Friends have mutual relationships with each other	God and humans have relationship of mutuality

We can see now that the metaphor of God as friend indicates a different relationship between God and humans than does the metaphor of God as father; the metaphor of friend highlights a mutual and trusting relationship between God and humans. If we were to map out more metaphors, we would begin to see even more ways of understanding the relationship between humans and God.

How we understand our relationship to God in turn affects how we understand ourselves. To use the metaphor of father once again, if we relate to God as children, we may begin to think of ourselves as child-like; this could include positive characteristics, such as wonder and joy, or more negative characteristics, such as a fear of punishment. Different metaphors for God highlight different aspects of God's relationship with humans and thus emphasize different characteristics that humans have. If we use just one metaphor, whether it is father or anything else, we are left with too narrow a perspective on what it means to be a human in relationship with God.

Just as employing multiple metaphors preserves a sense of God's mystery, so too does it preserve a sense of the mystery of being human. While our metaphors for God are only one of the many influences on theological anthropology, they can nonetheless have a powerful affect on our self-understandings. We do well to include many metaphors, both traditional and novel, when speaking of God; to do any less "fails both human beings and divine mystery."

The Four Sources

Thus far, I have showed some of the advantages of attending to more than one image of God. This approach both prevents one image of God from becoming hegemonic and offers more possibilities for understanding the human person, both in terms of understanding our relationship to God and in terms of the kinds of characteristics we understand ourselves to have. Some questions remain, however: Are all interpretations of the Trinity equally helpful? How do we know which images to use? In this section, I offer the four traditional sources for theological reflection—scripture, tradition, reason, and experience—as my primary methodological tool for gauging the fittingness of particular interpretations of the Trinity. Examining trinitarian interpretations and metaphors through the lens of the four sources offers a way to discover the strengths and weaknesses of different theologies. Using the four sources as a method recognizes that each source is too limited to stand on its own (e.g. sola scriptura); the more adequate theologies will draw from all four of the sources—scripture, tradition, reason, and experience—even if this means dealing with the tensions both within and among each of the sources.

In this section, I offer a brief explanation of each of the four sources. Then, in the following three chapters, I examine how John

Zizioulas, Elizabeth Johnson, and Catherine Keller employ each of these sources in their work in order to uncover the strengths and weaknesses of their interpretations of the Trinity. There is much to be said about each of the four sources individually. An exploration of just the questions and debates within biblical studies, for example, could fill volumes. I do not, then, intend to provide an exhaustive account of these sources. Rather, I will briefly show what I believe to be the central questions and contributions of each.

My own understanding of the four sources is drawn largely from Margaret Farley's definitions and use of them. Farley is a feminist Catholic ethicist who has written on a range of topics, including medical and sexual ethics. She also co-founded the All-Africa Conference, which brings together African women religious to develop strategies to more effectively address the HIV/AIDS crisis in sub-Saharan Africa. Below, I offer Farley's interpretation of the four sources. I also briefly show how she uses the sources herself as an example of how a feminist perspective affects one's interpretations and treatment of them.

Farley's approach to the four sources of scripture, tradition, reason, and experience is informed by her feminist commitments. Farley interprets feminism broadly as a movement to encourage the overall well-being of all women, yet she does not gloss over real differences among the women of the world. She advocates respect for all people and an awareness of their particular situations; she calls not for respect for a generalized other, but for a generalized respect for a specific other. Farley's feminist stance shapes what she values in each of the four sources and what she critiques. In general, Farley affirms the authority of each source, while at the same time hesitating to let one stand above the others. The four sources work with and inform one another. I begin with her understanding and use of the broadest source, reason.

REASON, OR SECULAR DISCIPLINES OF KNOWLEDGE

In her most recent book, *Just Love*, Farley has a brief section explaining each of the four sources. The first thing to notice is her understanding of reason. For her, reason as such is running through all of the sources; we use our reason to reflect on and engage the sources and to put them in conversation with each other. She thus renames the source of reason as "secular disciplines of knowledge." For her, this source includes every secular discipline that "offers the possibility of insight into the aspects of creation we seek to understand." In terms of sexual ethics, which *Just Love* addresses, these secular sources can include philosophy, biology, medicine, anthropology, and sociology, as well as literature and art. In general, the secular disciplines offer us a broad survey of human knowledge and can include any discipline. The sciences, for example, tell us about ourselves and our world, and this new knowledge informs our theologies so that they accurately reflect what we know about being human. The arts, literature, and poetry attest to the joys and heartbreak of our humanity, and they can powerfully affect how we see the world.

Although Farley has re-imagined this source as "secular disciplines on knowledge," the notion of "reason" itself is still important to consider. I focus on one particular issue here—the tendency to privilege reason over other aspects of our humanity, using Farley's reinterpretation of Kant as an example. Farley draws on Kant's second formulation of the categorical imperative—the formulation emphasizing respect for persons. Kant recognizes rational autonomy as the ground of this respect for persons; only a "rational being who obeys no law except the one which he himself also gives" has dignity. Respect for autonomy, for Kant, requires that we treat persons as ends in themselves and never as merely a means. Farley agrees with Kant's insistence that we treat humans as ends in themselves; "what is wrong with loving a person as a thing is that the person *is a person, not a thing.*" Farley, like Kant, recognizes that a person, as a self-determining agent, demands respect.

And yet for Farley, it is not simply our autonomy that requires respect, but also our relationality. She writes that human beings are essentially relational, with interpersonal and social needs and the ability to be open to others. We are persons not only in our freedom for self-determination, but also because we can move beyond ourselves through our capacity to love; "the capacity to love one another and all things…makes persons worthy of respect." To recognize another person's capacity to love and to see that person as loveable enables us to reach across lines of difference and to see other people as truly human and, as such, deserving of respect:

When we are caught up in the activity of loving, when love arises within us as a response to the beloved as worthy, valuable, loveable, just as when our gaze is held by the affliction of another such that both the observer and the sufferer are stripped of pretension and self-deceit, we find ourselves in the presence of what is genuinely human in the other.

Farley thus expands Kant's emphasis on rational autonomy as the ground of human dignity and identifies two "obligating features of personhood:" autonomy and relationality. Farley's emphasis on relationality brings in an affective dimension to the human person that is lacking in Kant. We bring our whole selves, not just the intellect, to our relationships with others and our decision-making.

Our autonomy is also bound up with our affections; we are not only free to choose a course of action, but also to choose loves and desires. Indeed, "every free choice ultimately includes a choice of what and how to love" For Farley, our affections and loves are not in opposition to our reason, but rather our reason helps us determine how to appropriately express our loves. Kant, on the other hand, insists on a sharp divide between reason and the emotions, claiming at one point that it is "only as intelligence" that we are properly human; in the sense that the affections have a heteronomous effect on the will, we cannot properly attribute them to our true selves. If I am subject to my inclinations, Kant would argue, I cannot be truly autonomous and cannot act as a moral agent. While Kant insists on a sharp divide between reason and the passions, with reason always in control, Farley recognizes that our lives are messier and more complex than that. There is no such thing, Farley writes, as complete control over the emotions by reason; such thinking rests on "a faulty model of the human self" and is blind to experience. Rather, we must respect our emotions as much as we respect our reason, even though they sometimes conflict. Our freedom of choice sometimes has a rocky relationship with our loves:

I know that I can choose my love, but not always. I can shape my love, but oh, so slowly. I can cultivate my love, but only through long and patient attention. I can discipline my love and liberate it; but sometimes it still slips through my heart or disrupts my ordered life.

Our affections are as much a part of our personhood as our reason, and we must value both equally. Only when we take our affections seriously, Farley argues, can we really learn how to love and how to properly respect other persons.

Our affections and desires, our reason, our vulnerability, our relationships, our powers of self-determination and freedom, our capacity to love—these are what make us worthy of respect and give us dignity. Farley's feminist account of the relationship between reason and the affective aspects of our lives gives us a much richer and satisfying understanding of ourselves than does Kant's. She shows us that "feminists may affirm autonomy, but need not thereby oppose freedom and affectivity, nor downplay human vulnerability, nor neglect individual histories of desire, social-historical situatedness, and communal formation." Although in the chapters that follow, I focus mainly on the theologians' use of secular disciplines of knowledge, I will also note how they understand reason and will pay attention to the affective aspects of their theologies and methods.

As I examine the theologies of John Zizioulas, Elizabeth Johnson, and Catherine Keller in the following three chapters, I ask the following questions about their own use of secular disciplines of knowledge:

What secular disciplines do they engage? Do they engage these disciplines in depth or cursorily? How does their use of secular disciplines inform or shape their arguments? Is their use of such disciplines consistent with a feminist perspective? How do they understand reason?

For Farley, the secular sources of knowledge are not absolute; they do not give us insight into "reality" as such, "but only a pragmatic way of dealing with the world and ourselves." Nonetheless, they offer important and meaningful insights and can help inform our theologies, when put in dialogue with the other sources of moral wisdom. It is to another of these sources, experience, that I now turn.

Experience

For Farley, experience is both the content of all the sources and is necessary for a coherent interpretation of each of them. "[E]xperience is essential for every form of knowledge," she writes, noting that even scripture and tradition are records and interpretations of people's experiences. Thus, the other sources are dependent on experience for their content. Farley defines experience as "the actual living of events and relationships, along with the sensations, feelings, images, emotions, insights, and understandings that are a part of this lived reality." Further, experience is both personal and social; we can have private and shared experiences. As an example, Farley writes specifically of the experience of God. In her discussion of experiencing God, she draws from James Gustafson's theocentric ethics, arguing for the place of the affections in our moral lives, as well as our ability to meet God in both our experiences of contingency and of beauty and order. Further following Gustafson, Farley argues that

a genuine experience of God, of an Ultimate Power, makes possible in and for us a decentering of ourselves and the human community in our understanding of the universe and even in our desires for its good. From this experience emerges the radical possibility of a Christian ethic that relativizes human well-being not only before God but before reality as a whole.

Our experience of God, then, can act as a check against anthropocentrism or domesticating God. When we experience our finitude and powerlessness, as well as when we are overwhelmed by beauty, we discover that God is much bigger than the box we might want to put God in. Thus, paying attention to our varied experiences can give us different perspectives on God and emphasizes the need for many metaphors for God to reflect these different experiences.

While experience can act as a helpful corrective and can help us interpret the other sources meaningfully, Farley notes, it is not without its flaws. Can we, for example, generalize about experience, since it is concrete and particular to persons or social groups? How much of our experience is socially constructed? Farley also admits that, as our lives progress, we give new meaning to our experiences. "We had the experience but missed the meaning," TS Eliot writes; when we approach an experience years later, we may find that it has a different meaning for us and thus that it shapes our theology or moral discernment differently. Yet, experience does not lose its value as a source because of this. Indeed, Farley argues, there are some things that we cannot know without experience, such as our own limitations, suffering, hope, and love. Our experiences shape who we are, and, even though it might complicate things, we must pay close attention to them when developing our theologies or making moral decisions.

As I explore the work of Zizioulas, Johnson, and Keller in the next three chapters, I ask the following questions about their use of experience as a source of knowledge: How do they understand the role of experience in shaping theological knowledge? How would they define experience? How, if at all, do they deal with the subjective nature of personal experience? How does their inclusion of experience shape their reasoning or arguments? Does their use of experience fit with a feminist perspective?

For Farley, experience is authoritative, but, like the secular disciplines, it does not hold sole authority: "Experience is subject to the Bible and to faith traditions; if it helps us to understand them, it nonetheless does so only insofar as it does not at the same time usurp their authority." Experience can correct, make intelligible, and interpret the other sources, but the same can be said for scripture, tradition, and the secular disciplines. I move now to the role of scripture in Farley's thought.

SCRIPTURE

For Farley, the biblical witness "claims to present a truth that will heal us, make us whole; it will free us, not enslave us to what violates our very sense of truth and justice." Further, she argues, if elements of scripture do not ring true to this sense of truth and goodness, they are not to be believed or accepted. The question to be asked of scripture, from Farley's feminist standpoint, is: "Is it a witness that is life-giving for women and for men, a witness that opens access to some truth that is freeing for all?"

Farley describes two fundamental beliefs of feminist consciousness that must be brought to bear on our interpretation of scripture. The first of these is the principle of equality; men and women are equally fully human and are to be treated as such. Women's claim to equality extends to an insistence on the equality of all people, especially those groups that have been marginalized. The second feminist principle Farley notes that bears on the interpretation of scripture is mutuality. This principle affirms the human person both in her autonomy and her relationality. Feminists, Farley argues, reject modes of relating that rely on competition and opposition and call instead for mutual respect. It is only through this principle of mutuality that human persons can "truly be affirmed as embodied subjects; as beings whose value lies not only in their freedom but also in their capacity to know and be known, to love and be loved; as beings whose destiny is communion." If aspects of the biblical witness contradict these principles of equality and mutuality, that is, if certain passages tend to the subjection of any group or fail to respect the full personhood of any group, they must be rejected or reinterpreted.

Farley, while noting difficulties with scripture as a source, does also affirm its usefulness for the Christian moral life. She argues that it can reveal moral principles, guidelines, and values, that it can motivate us by presenting a divine call and promise, that it can give meaning to our lives, help us to understand our human condition, and call us beyond ourselves to self-acceptance. For Farley, scripture is helpful in giving general guidelines and attitudes but not for giving specific codes of conduct.

James Gustafson's distinction between employing scripture as "revealed reality" and "revealed morality" is helpful here. Those who interpret scripture as "revealed morality" pull out specific moral norms from the Bible, while those who interpret it as "revealed reality" use scripture to interpret God's actions and understand some basic truths about humans and our relation to God. For Gustafson, scripture informs judgments about "what God is enabling and requiring man [*sic*] to be to and to do in particular natural, historical, and social circumstances," but it does not and cannot determine by itself what the actual judgments are to be. Scripture, for Gustafson, thus provides a basic orientation and perspective, but it is "never the final court of appeal for Christian ethics." Farley would agree.

As with the other sources, according to Farley, scripture's authority is not final; it must be corrected and interpreted through these other sources. Further, "without other sources of moral wisdom, the power of scripture cannot be mediated into the contemporary context." We must bring our own experience, our faith tradition, and the insights from the secular disciplines to our understanding of scripture if we are to make sense of it today, if we want it to speak truly to us in our own situation. In my analysis of the theologies of Zizioulas, Johnson, and Keller in chapters 3, 4, and 5, I ask the following questions about their use of scripture: What aspects of scripture do they privilege? Which texts have the most significance for them? How does their use of scripture inform or affect their overall arguments? Are their readings of scripture consonant with a feminist perspective? Do they understand scripture as revealed reality or revealed morality?

TRADITION

As with scripture and the other sources, Margaret Farley takes tradition seriously, yet she approaches it with a critical feminist eye. She emphasizes a "living" tradition, one that can grow and change; in a living tradition, "beliefs and the theologies that interpret beliefs can be challenged by new experiences, cultural shifts, and new perspectives on the past." She further argues that most theologians and ethicists allow room for the development of tradition. The question is how to "excavate historical layers of meaning, find lost treasures, take account of historical and cultural contexts for church life, hold on to gems of revelatory experience and shared faith." That is, what can stay, and what should go, and who decides? Broadly speaking, for Farley the tradition is a living one, one that grows along with the church, but yet is to be taken seriously as "revelatory of God's presence and action in the life of the community."

Farley engages tradition through the lens of her notion of just love. Justice, she writes, "requires that we affirm for persons, both women and men, what they reasonably need in order to live out their lives as full human persons and, within the Christian community, what they need in order to grow in the life of faith." A just love corresponds to the reality of the one loved and respects her full personhood, and any pattern of relationship that does not respect persons as such is unjust. Thus, Farley argues, the demand of a just love "makes for rejecting institutionalized gender differentiations and for affirming equality of opportunity for all persons regardless of their sex." Further, she argues, denying women their personal rights harms the common good; in the case of an all-male priesthood, she points out, not only are women not treated justly, but the whole church suffers because God is not fully represented and the life of faith fades. The tradition, then, she argues must be engaged from this standpoint of just love, and unjust patterns of relationship (especially, but not limited to, the relationship between women and men) should be rejected. Aspects of the tradition that deny equality, mutuality, and justice must, like similar elements of scripture, be rejected.

As an example, in an article called "Sources of Sexual Inequality in the History of Christian Thought," Farley views the Christian tradition with a critical feminist eye, aiming at "the possibilities of a theological reconstruction within the Christian tradition which may enable the church and the society it influences to move beyond patterns of relationship marked by sexual inequality to ones marked by equality." The question Farley asks in this essay is whether it is possible to cut out once and for all the roots of sexism in Christianity without destroying Christianity's very foundations; that is, is Christianity inherently sexist, or can parts of the tradition be recovered or transformed so that women can be viewed as equal to men? This is an important question for my purposes because I am working within the Christian tradition—specifically within trinitarian theology—to promote a liberatory and inclusive ethics. While Farley ultimately argues that the Christian tradition is not inherently unjust, she does note some deeply-rooted oppressive tendencies.

Farley points to two of the roots of sexism in Christian theology—the identification of women with evil and the identification of the fullness of the *imago Dei* only with men. In most patriarchal societies, she argues, women have been seen as a threat or temptation, "a source of disorder in the midst of a fragile order, a being capable of exposing and even of exploiting the vulnerability of the male person." Christianity was no exception. Theologians from Justin Martyr to Origen to Augustine to Thomas to Luther all portrayed Eve in some way as the seducer of Adam, such that the very idea of woman became entrenched in "sophisticated theologies of original sin, in anthropological theories of higher and lower nature, of mind and body, rationality and desire, and in spiritualistic eschatologies." The fear of women's sexuality and their bodies, Farley notes, was present before Christianity, but it was solidified through theological arguments.

A second strand in the Christian tradition that Farley points to as a source of sexism is the idea that only men are fully in the *imago Dei*, a strand that she argues is less explicit but more devastating; "[i]t is not only in the order of sin but in the order of nature and the order of grace that women have been declared lesser than men." This identification of the male with the *imago Dei* has its roots in our understanding of God:

The Old Testament presented a God who was, in contradistinction to the gods of other peoples, most importantly a transcendent god. Yahweh was no earth-goddess; his creation was not a matter of earthen fertility...Wholly transcendent, he was neither male nor female. But when a human analogue was looked for, it was clear that for the Hebrews such transcendence could be portrayed only in masculine terms. It was, after all, masculinity that connoted strength in relation to feminine weakness, activity in relation to passivity, fullness in relation to emptiness, autonomy in relation to dependence. The doctrine of God and the doctrine of the human person were already inextricably intertwined.

The fullness of the image of God, then, was seen to reside in the man, with women participating only to a degree. This, Farley, argues, has had far-reaching consequences. Men came to be seen as representatives of God, since they were fully in God's image, while women were merely lovers of God. Thus, women have been excluded from a full share in the ministry of the church. Here we see again the importance of opening up our images of God and including non-masculine metaphors. The traditional language for the Trinity—Father, Son, and Holy Spirit—can and does have direct implications for the way the church itself is structured. In the chapters that follow, I will pay attention to how Zizioulas, Keller, and Johnson understand and employ this traditional language and whether they are open to using other metaphors.

Farley respects the authority of tradition, yet she examines it carefully and with a critical eye. She admits to being "aghast at what I found coming from some of the greatest minds in Western history," yet rather than rejecting tradition out of hand, she points to aspects of it that have not been emphasized and calls for the transformation of those aspects of it that have been problematic. As I examine the theologies of Zizioulas, Johnson, and Keller in the following three chapters, I ask these questions about their use of tradition: How do they interpret the meaning of tradition? What aspects of tradition do they privilege? How does their use of tradition inform their projects? Is their use of tradition consistent with a feminist perspective that privileges equality, justice, and mutuality?

USING ALL FOUR SOURCES

In this section, I have overviewed the four sources of secular disciplines of knowledge, experience, scripture, and tradition. Each of the sources is authoritative, yet only in relation to the authority of the other sources; this leads necessarily to dialogue between the sources rather than a dictatorship of one over the others. Margaret Farley brings the broad base of the secular disciplines of knowledge and the insights gained from experience to bear on the aspects of scripture and tradition that are not in keeping with her commitments to feminism and to just love. Farley's feminist commitments and her "stance" of just love inform how she approaches each of the sources. Anything, in any of the sources, that promotes unjust patterns of relationship, subjugates women to men, or does not respect persons as such needs to be reconsidered and reinterpreted.

I also keep these commitments in mind as I examine the theologies of John Zizioulas, Catherine Keller, and Elizabeth Johnson in the chapters that follow. In these chapters, I use the four sources as my primary methodological tool for examining and critiquing these theologians' interpretations of the Trinity. Examining their use of the four sources will allow me to uncover the strengths and the weaknesses of their theologies. I consider not only their use of each particular source but also the ways in which they allow the sources to inform each other and whether they employ the sources equally or prefer one or two over the others. Because I use these theologies to suggest implications for human life, it will be important to have evaluated them and to be aware of their strengths and weaknesses. I will mainly use the strengths of each of the images in pulling out implications for humans, but the weaknesses of the images remind us that none is perfect or can capture the full reality of either God or humanity. The methodological use of the four sources suggests a way to compare different interpretations of God; those theologies that employ all of the sources in creative, thoughtful, and critical ways should tend to produce better interpretations of God.

Looking Forward

In this chapter I have shown some effects and implications of metaphorical language for God. I have argued that employing multiple metaphors better captures our experience of and relationship to God. Attending to a variety of metaphors both preserves a sense of God's mystery and offers more ways to imagine the relationship between God and humans and the kinds of characteristics of God that humans can also embody. I also offered Margaret Farley's feminist interpretation of the four sources of secular disciplines, experience, tradition, and scripture as a way of gauging the suitability of particular understandings of God.

In the next three chapters, I explore three of these understandings of God and the ways in which they can affect how humans understand themselves and the kinds of virtues they want to embody. Chapter 3 examines the theology of John Zizioulas, a Greek Orthodox theologian; Chapter 4 examines the theology of Elizabeth Johnson, a Roman Catholic feminist theologian; and Chapter 5 examines the theology of Catherine Keller, a Protestant process theologian. Each of these three chapters follows the same structure: 1) Overview and evaluation of the interpretation of the Trinity through the lens of the four sources, 2) Implications of the interpretation of God for theological anthropology 3) Uncovering a virtue implicit in the theology 4) Example of how the virtue can be applied.

3

The Theology of John Zizioulas

"Grown-ups love figures. When you tell them that you have made a new friend, they never ask you any questions about essential matters. They never say to you, 'What does his voice sound like? What games does he love best? Does he collect butterflies?' Instead, they demand, 'How old is he? How many brothers has he? How much does he weigh? How much money does his father make?' Only from these figures do they think that they have learned anything about him."

--*The Little Prince,* Antoine de Saint Exupéry

The underlying belief of this dissertation is that the metaphors we use for God and the ways in which we interpret God can affect our entire worldview, including our understanding of ourselves. In the last chapter, I showed the importance of employing multiple interpretations of God so that both our theologies and our anthropologies remain fresh and open. In this chapter, and in the two that follow, I begin to explore in more depth the effects that particular interpretations of the Trinity can have on our understanding of who we are and who we want to become. In this chapter, I examine the theology of Greek Orthodox theologian John Zizioulas, whose emphasis on personhood celebrates otherness and relationality in both God and humans.

John Zizioulas was born in 1931 and began his theological education in 1950 at the universities of Thessalonika and Athens. In 1955,
he left for the United States to study at Harvard. While there, he
studied patristics with Georges Florovsky, a Russian Orthodox theologian, and philosophy with Paul Tillich. He received his doctorate
from the University of Athens in 1966. He was consecrated a bishop
in 1986 and is currently the titular Metropolitan of Pergamon. In
addition to his work on the Trinity and personhood, Zizioulas has
also written on ecclesiology, and he has been an active member in
ecumenical dialogue. In addition to having worked with the World
Council of Churches, he was a founding member in 1979 of the International Joint Commission for Theological Dialogue with the Roman
Catholic Church and is also co-chairman of the international Angli-
can-Orthodox dialogue. Zizioulas is also known for his work on the
environment, especially his lecture series entitled "Preserving God's
Creation," given at King's College, London in 1989. In all of these
matters, John Zizioulas has called his fellow Orthodox Christians to
not simply engage in debate about doctrine but to work to bring to
light the existential and ethical implications of their beliefs.

For my purposes, I look at one aspect of John Zizioulas' work—the
Trinity—and the implications it has for human life. Zizioulas establishes a relational ontology, stressing that relationality is the heart of
being itself, which intends to preserve both the oneness of the biblical God and the multiplicity implied by the doctrine of the Trinity.
For him, "person" is a relational term; one is not a person without
relationship. Thus, Zizioulas would argue, when we think of the *one
person*, God the Father, we immediately call to mind the Father's *relationships* with the Son and the Spirit; the Father's relation to the Son
and the Spirit are constitutive of his personhood.

In my examination of Zizioulas' trinitarian theology, I bracket off
much of his other work to focus on his interpretation of the Trinity
and the language and metaphors he uses for God. As I indicated in
the previous chapter, I will examine his understanding of the Trin-

ity through the four sources of tradition, scripture, secular disciplines of knowledge, and experience. In this examination, the central features of his theology will emerge, and I will be able to determine its strengths and weaknesses. Following this examination of his trinitarian theology, I will then turn to its existential and ethical implications, offering an exploration of Zizioulas' theological anthropology and offering a virtue—wonder—that emerges from his theology. Finally, I show how this virtue might be applied in everyday situations. I begin with an examination of Zizioulas' trinitarian theology through his use of the four sources. I look primarily at those parts of his work that deal explicitly with the Trinity; this is not meant to be a complete or exhaustive account of his use of the four sources.

Zizioulas' Use of the Four Sources

TRADITION

Of the four sources, Zizioulas relies most heavily on tradition. His use of tradition focuses mainly on his interpretation of the contributions of the Cappadocian fathers. Cappadocia lies in what is now Turkey and in the first few centuries of Christianity became an important center of Christian theology. It was home to four major thinkers—known as a group as the Cappadocian fathers—who, according to Zizioulas, initiated "a radical reorientation of classical Greek humanism" and a major breakthrough in trinitarian theology. These thinkers were Basil the Great (c. 330-79), his younger brother Gregory of Nyssa (c. 335-94), Gregory of Nazianzus (c. 330-89), and his cousin Amphilocus (340/45-?).

Zizioulas outlines several contributions the Cappadocians made to trinitarian theology. I highlight two below—the monarchy of the Father and the understanding of "person." First, Zizioulas notes the Cappadocian contribution of the monarchy of the Father as a way to emphasize both the unity and the relationality of the Trinity. He emphasizes that the term "monarchy" today has implications that it did not have for the Cappadocians; today a monarchy suggests one ruler who exercises power over the rest of the population. While the word "monarchy" does come from the Greek for "one rule or power," it is perhaps best rendered "one cause." The monarchy of the Father, Zizioulas argues, does not mean that the Father exercises power over the Son and the Spirit, but rather that the Father is the *one cause*, in the sense of "personal ontological origination," of the three persons of the Trinity. It was "the *one*, the Father, that 'moved' to threeness," according to Gregory of Nazianzus.

Zizioulas further elaborates on this idea of the Father as "cause" of divine threeness, based mainly on his reading of Gregory of Nazianzus. He first notes that the Father's movement into threeness happens before and outside time, so that the Son and the Spirit cannot be understood to come "after" the Father, temporally speaking. He also notes that the Father as cause implies freedom and love; "divine love constitutes divine being in a *personal* way." For him, love is a gift, freely given, coming from another (in this case the Father) that affirms the Son's and the Spirit's uniqueness. The person of the Father freely, and thus out of love, chooses to move into threeness and into a relationship with the Son and the Holy Spirit. As he puts it, "*He, as a particular being*, (the Father) brings about his own being (the Trinity)." At the same time that the Father freely enters these relationships, he also gives personhood to the Son and the Spirit, transmitting "personal otherness." Zizioulas thus argues that the Cappadocian theology is able to hold both the primacy of the Father as cause and the equality of the three persons of the Trinity; "the 'cause' of a personal identity brings forth, 'causes,' fully other, that is, ontologically free and fully equal, identities. A-symmetry is not, therefore, incompatible with equality." The monarchy of the Father, as Zizioulas sees it, suggests that the Trinity emerges not out of substance but out of the freedom and love, that is the *person*, of the Father.

Thus, Zizioulas also notes the importance of the term "person" as the Cappadocians used it. For him, "person" is a relational term; to speak of a person means to speak both of unique identity and relationality. When we speak of the Father, then, we speak also of the Son and the Spirit—those divine persons with whom the Father has initiated a relationship. The Cappadocian concept of person emerged in dialogue with other theologies of the 4th century, particularly Sabellianism and Eunomianism. Sabellianism offered an understanding of the Trinity in which the three members of the Trinity were not persons but rather roles assumed by the one God. Zizioulas notes that Sabellius implied that there was one person, not three, in God, thereby neglecting to take intra-divine relationality into account. The Cappadocians, on the other hand, stressed three persons in God, arguing for the "fullness and integrity of each person." In other words, they stressed the threeness of God over the oneness, emphasizing that the three come into communion because of the person of the Father.

Eunomianism suggested that the substance of God is unbegottenness, and that, because the Son was 'begotten,' he was not a part of the substance of God. Zizioulas notes that Eunomianism was a more philosophically sophisticated version of Arianism, which argued that the Son was created and thus not fully God. Part of the Cappadocian response to this theology was to emphasize that 'unbegottenness' was a property of the person of the Father, and not of the substance of God. Because a divine person is defined through properties that are *unique*, we know the Father precisely through his unbegottenness, and the Son through his begottenness. By attributing these qualities to personhood, the Cappadocians underscored "the idea that personhood can be known and identified through its absolute uniqueness and irreplaceability." Thus the Cappadocians showed that the Son's absolute difference from the Father did not make him less than God but rather a person—equal to and in relationship with the Father.

Though he relies on them heavily, Zizioulas' interpretation of the Cappadocians has been a subject of some debate; some thinkers have argued that he reads modern existential philosophy back into the Cappadocians' writings, thus misinterpreting them. Lucian Turcescu, for example, has argued that modern western thinkers such as Martin Buber, John Macmurray, and David Jenkins have colored Zizioulas' interpretations especially of Gregory of Nyssa and Basil of Caesarea. Turcescu argues that Gregory and Basil do not distinguish between "person" (understood as relational) and "individual" (understood as self-contained), and that they, therefore, do not in fact have a relational ontology. "Despite claiming that his own ontology of personhood is patristic-based," Turcescu argues, "Zizioulas has not convincingly exegeted the Cappadocian theology of person" and has instead foisted nineteenth- and twentieth-century insights onto the Cappadocians.

Aristotle Papanikolau, however, suggests that Turcescu overlooks the prominent role of Gregory of Nazianzus in Zizioulas' work. Papanikolau argues that Gregory of Nazianzus contributed the most to the understanding of the monarchy of the Father that is so important to Zizioulas. According to Papanikolau, whether or not the Cappadocians distinguish between "person" and "individual" matters much less for a relational ontology of personhood than does the monarchy of the Father; "if there is an ontology that is personal and relational, in which person has ontological priority over substance, it is because of the monarchy of the Father." Thus, Papanikolau suggests, we can conclude that Zizioulas' relational ontology is sufficiently grounded in tradition and that he is not in fact an existentialist in disguise.

Why does it matter whether Zizioulas' theology is grounded in patristic theology or in existential philosophy? It is not my intention to settle the argument. Rather, the debate over Zizioulas' interpretation of the Cappadocians shows the enduring importance and relevance of tradition in theological reflection; tradition ties us to the ideas and experiences of those who have come before us. The most important aspects of Zizioulas' theology, such as the understanding of personhood as relational and the Father as cause, emerge from his reading of the tradition. Yet tradition is not the only source, and as we will soon see, Zizioulas also engages scripture, experience, and secular disciplines of knowledge. The arguments of some of Zizioulas' critics imply that tradition matters more than the other sources, but Papanikolau (and Zizioulas himself) argues that the other sources are necessary: "The alternative [to employing other sources] is either the hermeneutically impossible bracketing of all that the interpreter has read and experienced as they approach the patristic texts in the hope of distilling the pure 'essence' of the text itself; or to judge contemporary Orthodox theology as authentic based on its faithful reiteration of patristic texts, i.e., a form of patristic fundamentalism." In other words, while it may be a helpful task to determine whether Zizioulas interprets the Cappadocian texts appropriately, it is not a weakness that he does also enlist the help of modern philosophy and other sources of knowledge in constructing his theology. I turn now to his use of scripture in that endeavor.

SCRIPTURE

Zizioulas relies less heavily on scripture than on tradition in making his arguments, but he chooses to employ the aspects of tradition he does in part because they are the truest to scripture. For example, he privileges Gregory of Nazianzus' understanding of the monarchy of the Father because it best preserves biblical monotheism and the language of "God the Father." Zizioulas cites several instances in the New Testament, especially in the letters of Paul, in which the phrase "God the Father" is used, arguing that "this is how God calls and indicates himself in revealing himself to us" throughout scripture. He also suggests, referencing Matthew 28:19, that the origin of the phrase is baptismal and that "the idea of God as Father did not arise as speculative reflection about God, but emerged from ecclesial experience." Thus, Zizioulas argues, the understanding of the one God as Father has strong biblical and early ecclesial roots and ought to be preserved; "if we allow for anything beyond the Father as ultimate reality, we must bear in mind that biblical monotheism is at stake."

He further argues that much of western theology, especially Augustine, moved away from these biblical roots by emphasizing the oneness of the substance of the Trinity over the person of the Father; it was no longer one God, the Father, but one God, the Trinity, which meant "a radical departure from the biblical association with God the Father." The desire to preserve biblical monotheism is in part why Zizioulas prefers the Cappadocian interpretation of the monarchy of the Father. Not only does this position emphasize the freedom and personhood of the Father, but it also preserves biblical monotheism by understanding the Father as the single source of the personhood of the Son and the Spirit. Here Zizioulas' relational ontology comes into play; when we call God "Father," we not only respect the biblical tradition but also, because the Father, as a person, is essentially relational, we also immediately call to mind his relations with the other members of the Trinity. In other words, the Father "remains the God of the Bible by being the ground of unity of the three persons."

Zizioulas also relies on the biblical understanding of God as love (1 John 4:16). It is out of love that the Father moves to threeness; love is "constitutive of his substance" and identified with freedom. The Father's love impels him outward into communion with the Son and the Spirit. Because this movement is done out of love, it is done freely. Thus, Zizioulas' understanding of the Father as 'cause' of divine threeness is consistent with the scriptural belief that God is love. Other than his desire to preserve the biblical understanding of the one God as Father and God as love, Zizioulas does not make much use of scripture. He relies far more on tradition, citing scripture occasionally to show how it fits with his interpretation of the tradition. Though he does not rely heavily on scripture to make his arguments, we can see that remaining true to scripture is nonetheless important for Zizioulas because he chooses to emphasize aspects of the tradition that are consistent with his interpretation of scripture.

SECULAR DISCIPLINES OF KNOWLEDGE

Of the secular disciplines, Zizioulas makes the most use of philosophy, with which he has a complicated relationship. As we saw above, Zizioulas has been accused of "attempting to dress his philosophical personalism and existentialism with Cappadocian language and parade it as patristic." Setting aside the question of Zizioulas' interpretation of the Cappadocians, it is clear that he does engage the writings of nineteenth- and twentieth-century philosophers, as well as ancient Greek philosophers. His engagement with both ancient and modern philosophy centers mostly around understandings of self and personhood. His engagement with philosophy typically tends to highlight the merits of theological understandings of the person, but he does not reject philosophy out of hand. For example, in *Communion and Otherness*, Zizioulas overviews understandings of the self and otherness in western philosophical thought, engaging such thinkers as Husserl, Heidegger, Levinas, and Buber. While he ultimately rejects each of their understandings of the self in favor of the more theological interpretation of the Cappadocians, he nonetheless argues that "any attempt to question the idea of self at a philosophical level should be applauded." Zizioulas appreciates the contribution of these philosophers, and asks many of the same questions that they raise: What is the self? What is a person? Who is the 'other?' Is relationality threatening or affirming? Though many of the questions are similar, in the end, Zizioulas chooses theological answers over philosophical ones.

In his engagement with both ancient and modern philosophy, Zizioulas is careful to emphasize the priority of theology over philosophy; philosophical ideas can be used to help shed light on theological insights, but theology is not dependent on philosophy. Yet for Zizioulas, "to be in dialogue with modern philosophy and discover points of convergence, as well as fundamental differences," is a suitable task for theologians. For him, the main difference is that philosophy starts with the human and theology starts with God; although there may be similarities between Zizioulas' understanding of the person and modern existentialist philosophy, ultimately, he argues, the difference is that his understanding of the person is based on the Trinity and not observations about humanity.

EXPERIENCE

Zizioulas explores experience at a general level, reflecting on such experiences as love and mortality. Because his discussion of these experiences relates more to the human person than to his understanding of God, I explore his understanding of love and mortality in more detail in the next section on theological anthropology. As we will see then, the experience of love is one that is common to both God and humanity, but the experience of mortality introduces important distinctions between human and divine persons.

In terms of his specifically trinitarian reflections, Zizioulas engages experience the least out of the four sources. It is possible that he interprets tradition as the recorded experiences of the early church, or that our experiences of God reveal what it truly means to be a person, but he himself does not explicitly indicate this. Zizioulas' work on the Trinity is dominated by his use of the patristic tradition; he does engage scripture, secular disciplines, and experience, but the most salient aspects of his trinitarian theology are drawn from tradition.

A FEMINIST PERSPECTIVE ON ZIZIOULAS' USE OF THE FOUR SOURCES

As I indicated in the last chapter, I am examining Zizioulas' use of the four sources not only in terms of the extent to which he employs them and the aspects of each that he chooses to emphasize but also from a feminist perspective. As we saw, Margaret Farley questions aspects of each of the sources that do not promote women's liberation and that threaten justice and mutuality. How does Zizioulas fare from a feminist standpoint? Some aspects of his theology are consistent with Farley's feminist commitments; others are not.

As we have seen, Zizioulas relies heavily on the Christian tradition, especially the contributions of the Cappadocian fathers, in presenting his own understanding of the Trinity. Zizioulas argues that the Cappadocians offered an understanding of personhood that emphasizes both freedom and relationality. His reliance on tradition, however, could leave him open to criticism. For example, he continues to exclusively use the traditional trinitarian language of Father, Son, and Holy Spirit. As we saw in the previous chapter, such language can become reified and stale. Further, Zizioulas responds to feminist critiques of exclusively male God-language by arguing that the divine Fatherhood is not at all analogous to human fatherhood because human fathers exist individually before their children, whereas the divine Father, although the source of his personal being, exists only in relation to the Son. That is, in humans, individuality precedes communion, whereas in the divine persons, individuality and communion always exist together, outside of time. Zizioulas further argues that "all fears that by maintaining the biblical language of God the Father we encourage sexism in religion and society are dissolved in such a relational ontology. The Fatherhood of God is incompatible with individualism and, therefore, with notions of oppression, and so on."

It would seem, then, that Zizioulas does not understand our language for God to be metaphorical. Rather, the terms suggest personal ontological uniqueness such that calling the Father anything but 'Father' threatens that uniqueness and confuses the relationships among the persons of the Trinity. As we saw in the previous chapter, many feminist theologians have insisted that all theological language is metaphorical and that it is irresponsible to use only one set of terms for the Trinity. Zizioulas insists that the person of the Father has revealed himself to us as such and that we ought therefore call him 'Father' and only 'Father', while feminist theologians point to the oppressive and hegemonic tendencies of such an exercise. This is perhaps where Zizioulas' theology is most inconsistent with a feminist perspective.

Zizioulas' understanding of the monarchy of the Father could also draw criticism from a feminist perspective. Some might argue that it builds hierarchy into the Trinity and that a similar hierarchy thus shows up in the church. Zizioulas would counter that, although the Father is ontologically prior to the Son and the Spirit, he is not "higher up" because, at the same time that the Father causes the Son and the Spirit to be, his own personhood depends on the relationships he has with them. Zizioulas' understanding of the monarchy of the Father is a very nuanced position that is open to misinterpretation. He writes, for example, that, "in the Holy Trinity, the Father is 'greater,' precisely while generating others of full an equal ontological status." The question is, then, is the Father's 'greater-ness' truly consistent with full equality?

A final point of possible contention between Zizioulas and feminist theologians is his use (or lack thereof) of experience. The role of experience in theological reflection will become clearer in the next chapters, as I examine the theologies of Elizabeth Johnson and Catherine Keller, two feminist theologians. As I indicated in the previous chapter, employing experience as a source can be difficult because it is often subjective and open to interpretation. Nonetheless, it remains an important source of knowledge about ourselves, the world, and God. Zizioulas does not allow for different perspectives on the Trinity based on different experiences, such as the experience of women or other marginalized groups. He also does not seem to allow for different individual ways of experiencing God; rather, God is who he has revealed himself to be, and personal experiences of God matter less than what the traditional interpretation, based on the communal experience of God, gives us.

Though Zizioulas' heavy reliance on tradition, non-metaphoric use of God-language, and lack of attention to experience would all draw criticism from feminist theologians, other aspects of his theology would elicit their praise. For example, his insistence on the essentially relational and loving nature of God is consistent with most feminist theologies. His emphasis on uniqueness and particularity would also fit well with feminist commitments, especially in terms of the anthropological implications of Zizioulas' understanding of the Trinity. Examining Zizioulas' theology through the four sources has allowed us to uncover its possible weaknesses and its strengths. In the next section, I show what Zizioulas' interpretation of the Trinity suggests about human beings.

Anthropological Implications of Zizioulas' Theology

"Each individual is a miracle. No wonder we go on speaking of the dead for twenty years."

-Antoine de Saint-Exupéry, *Wind, Sand, and Stars*

The anthropological implications of Zizioulas' work on the Trinity center around the notion of personhood, and he himself is clear about both the similarities and the differences between divine and human personhood. What we have learned from his discussion of the Trinity is that in divine personhood, "otherness is *constitutive* of unity, and not consequent upon it. God is not first one and then three, but simultaneously one and three." Each of the divine persons remains unique and distinct while also being in communion with each of the others; otherness and communion coincide. As Catherine LaCugna put it, "only *in communion* can God be what God is, and only *as communion* can God be at all." Personhood, then, implies both otherness and relationship, "a particularity established in and through *communion*." In understanding the divine persons in such a way, Zizioulas argues, we can also learn something about human persons; we too are particular and distinct, yet we do not truly exist apart from our relationships with others. Based on his understanding of divine personhood, Zizioulas argues for the same relational ontology that will define the human person as essentially relational and absolutely unique.

Zizioulas rejects notions of the self that understand the person as an autonomous individual, arguing instead that relationality is the constitutive element not only of divine but also of human personhood: "the person cannot be conceived in itself as a static entity, but only as it *relates* to." He thus opposes Boethius' understanding of person as *naturae rationalis individua substantia* ("individual substance of a rational nature") and Descartes' *res cogitans* ("thinking thing"), since these suggest a rational, isolated individual. For him, one is not a person because one has reason but because one relates—to oneself, to others, and to God. This opens up ways of being a person that do not depend on rationality:

To be a person on this account is to be what one gives to and receives freely from the other persons with whom one is in relation. It is also to be noted that, unlike many individualistic modern conceptions of the person rooted in reason or consciousness, it does not exclude—for example—the mentally handicapped from personhood: like other persons, they too are what they are in giving and receiving, although the particular content of their giving and receiving will differ from that of others.

It is the nature of a person to be constantly relating to beings outside oneself; "personhood implies the openness of being, and even more than that, the *ek-stasis* of being, that is, a movement towards communion which leads to a transcendence of the boundaries of the 'self.'" Just as the person of God the Father moves into threeness, so too are human persons called to move out of themselves and into relationship. Here again Zizioulas' distinction between person and individual is important. As Patricia Fox puts it, "to become fully a person, ecstatically and hypostatically, is to break through the isolating boundaries of individualism into a life of inclusive communion with persons valued for their uniqueness and differences."

In addition to this relational ontology, Zizioulas argues also for the ontological uniqueness of every person, divine and human. It is, for him, through relationships with unique others that we recognize our own unique identities. In trinitarian terms, the Father is uniquely Father because of, *not in spite of*, his relationship with the Son and the Spirit; so too are humans constituted as unique persons *because of* their relationality. Further, Zizioulas argues, because this uniqueness resides at the level of being itself, that is, at the ontological level, persons cannot be judged on their accidental qualities, such as gender, good looks, or moral goodness. For Zizioulas, the Other remains absolutely particular and unique, resisting all generalization because "he or she would cease to be truly Other if placed in a class or category applicable to more than one entity. By being a person, the Other is by definition unique and therefore unclassifiable." By making uniqueness ontological, Zizioulas prevents us from generalizing about or categorizing groups of people. In short, "the constitutive elements of personhood [both human and divine] are self-affirmation in freedom and not necessity; the affirmation by another in love; uniqueness, concreteness, and unrepeatability; subsistence in communion."

The human person, however, unlike the divine persons, is created, contingent, and fallen. We are unable to have a true ontology of communion because "the world ultimately consists of a fragmented existence in which beings are particular *before* they can relate to each other: you first *are* and then relate." That is, we must first establish that we exist, and only then relate. Our *communion* is subsequent to our *being*, whereas in the Trinity, they are simultaneous. Further, the relationships in the Trinity are eternal, whereas ours are cut short by death. In the following section, I elaborate on how Zizioulas understands human personhood to differ from divine personhood, focusing primarily on human mortality.

PERSONHOOD AND DEATH

Death, Zizioulas writes, "is the threatening of being with non-being, the possibility that personhood may be turned into thinghood." As created beings, humans both come into existence and cease to exist; we are born and we die, and when those close to us die, our relationships with them are broken. If, as Zizioulas insists, our personhood is bound up with our relationships, then death threatens that personhood. He suggests that death sacrifices the person to nature; the cycles of birth and death ensure the survival of the species, of human *nature*, but at the expense of *particular* human persons. Because we are created and contingent, Zizioulas argues, "nature not only precedes particular beings and dictates its laws to them, but also finally swallows them up through death. From the point of view of nature, the particular being has no hope for survival and ever-being." Though the human species will survive and continue, I myself will not.

And yet, for Zizioulas, it is only as a particular being that I am capable of communion, relationship, and uniqueness; particularity makes my personhood possible. Thus, when a particular human being near us dies, it strikes us as odd or unacceptable. Death destroys the particular, and thus threatens our very being:

Particularity is built into ontology in such a way as to make it not just absurd to the mind but existentially unacceptable that any body with which we relate, establishing through this relationship our own particular being, should die and disappear. The death of a body may be nature's way of surviving, but the survival of the particular being is just as important in existence.

We thus begin to feel death should not happen to us, if we are to be truly persons. Death sacrifices our particularity to the processes of nature, and though we might cry out in protest, our own deaths are inescapable.

Love also is bound up with our particularity, since it is only in communion that we fully realize our otherness. We can only love what is particular. In a footnote, Zizioulas points to Antoine de Saint-Exupéry's *The Little Prince* as an example of an "ontology of love." In this book, the little prince learns that only those creatures we tame—establish particular ties with—can we truly love. The little prince meets a fox who teaches him about taming. The fox tells him, "If you tame me, then we shall need each other. To me, you will be

unique in all the world. To you, I shall be unique in all the world."
By alluding to the little prince, Zizioulas indicates that we can only be
loved when we are seen as particular and unique:

"[O]utside the communion of love the person loses its uniqueness
and becomes a being like other beings, a 'thing' without absolute
'identity' and 'name,' without a face. Death for a person means ceasing
to love and to be loved, ceasing to be unique and unrepeatable,
whereas life for the person means the survival of the uniqueness of its
hypostasis, which is affirmed and maintained by love."

Thus the problem is exacerbated: death, in threatening our relationality, destroys also our particularity, and thus our ability to be
loved.

The problem of our deaths, Zizioulas further notes, begins at our
birth. We are born into a finite, contingent, mortal existence; "birth
by normal procreation...is for created beings a cause of individualiza-
tion and is thus a birth of beings destined to death." Thus the very
process of procreation and bringing forth new life is at the same
time the process of bringing about death. Human sexuality, Zizioulas
claims, serves nature at the expense of the person, "something that the
person as the particular *par excellence* refuses to accept. This is why
the birth of a particular human being, being as it is the product of a
mechanism of death, cannot but lead into a conflict between person
and nature at the ontological level." How, then, are we to be persons,
if our inescapable mortality threatens our communion with others
and our own unique particularity? Simply as natural human beings, it
seems, we have no hope of true personhood, destined as we are for
death, that trampling over of personhood by nature. Indeed, Zizioulas
argues, "the person you love as unique cannot maintain his ontological uniqueness, cannot be truly unique, if death overcomes him in the
end. He can be truly unique only in him who has conquered death." It
is, he argues, only in Christ, through Baptism, that the possibility of
true personhood opens up to us.

The question raised in the preceding paragraphs is this: Human personhood, like divine personhood, is defined by our absolute uniqueness and communion with others, yet death, a reality for humans but not God, threatens our relationships and our uniqueness, so how can we truly be persons? Zizioulas locates the answer in the church community, and in the sacrament of Baptism in particular. If death destroys our personhood, it is thus only by conquering death that we can save our personhood. Further, Zizioulas argues, we are created 'in the image and likeness of God', which means that our particularities should be "ontologically true, like the persons of the holy Trinity, that is, not subject to disappearance and death." The divine persons are persons precisely because their relationships are eternal and not threatened by death. Our relationships, and thus our personhood, are destroyed by death. In short, in order to ensure the survival of our personhood, we need a 'new birth' that gives us not just life, but everlasting life, a birth that does not destine us for death, but only for true life. This is the 'new birth' of Baptism. Through natural birth, nature overtakes the person; through the 'new birth' of Baptism, "the person has the final word over nature." It is, for Zizioulas, through Baptism in Christ that we are guaranteed uniqueness and enduring personhood.

And yet, although we have been 'born again' into eternal life through Baptism, we nonetheless remain created and contingent; we are still going to die. How do we reconcile our 'new life' with our old one? Zizioulas comments:

"[T]his identity [acquired in Baptism] can never be fully realized in history as long as nature still dictates is laws to man, particularly in the form of death. When death ceases to be 'natural,' humanity will experience the true ontology of the person. Meanwhile, man is called to fulfill the image of God in him as much as possible, striving to free himself from the necessity of nature, experiencing 'sacramentally' the 'new being' as a member of the community of those 'born again' (in the above sense), and maintaining an eschatological vision and expectation of the transformation of the world."

Our Baptism, then, offers the hope of enduring personhood, a hope that finds its ground in the resurrection, which signifies the final triumph of life over death. Human beings will continue to die; yet, Zizioulas argues, we now have been given hope that our personhood will not be destroyed, that through Baptism we will die with Christ in order to rise with Him. In the meantime, while the possibility of everlasting life and personhood lies dormant in us, and while we continue on as contingent and mortal beings, we are to live in hope, looking always forward to the eschaton, while striving ever more diligently here and now to realize, as much as we can, our own personhood and the personhood of those around us. Zizioulas thus sees both commonalities and differences between divine and human personhood. Both are relational and emphasize particularity. Yet human mortality breaks relationships, threatening personhood; the only solution lies in Christ's conquering of death and our participation in that through Baptism.

CRITIQUES OF ZIZIOULAS' ANTHROPOLOGY

Zizioulas has drawn criticism of some aspects of his theological anthropology, most notably for a lack of attention to bodily experience and an over-reliance on ecclesiology. First, Zizioulas has drawn criticism for undervaluing bodily experience. Although his insistence on the absolute ontological uniqueness of each person prevents us from judging people based on certain accidental qualities, such as social status, good looks, or age, it also tends to eclipse other creaturely experiences that could contribute to our understanding of what it means to be a person. Alan Torrance, for example has asked how Zizioulas' exclusively ontological account of personhood can

take account of the hard realities of suffering, alienation, and separation—not only through death, but as a result of physical, social, economic, and other factors—of cerebral disintegration through age, mental handicap and so on? Are we not compelled to take these factors seriously as ontologically *constitutive* of personal, creaturely identity?"

This suggests that Zizioulas does not take adequate account of bodily factors such as suffering or of the social and historical situatedness of human beings and the ways in which we are shaped by culture and institutions. Torrance argues that Zizioulas "has a tendency to want to escape bodily constraints" by grounding his account of the human person in an idealized ontology.

Catherine LaCugna has also noted Zizioulas' lack of attention to the realities of human life. She notes that "not every configuration of persons-in-relation images God." While Zizioulas does attend to the reality of death, perhaps he could attend more carefully to the ways in which his theology and anthropology neglect to deal with human suffering, systems of exploitation or domination, and the ways in which our relationships can fail to respect the freedom and uniqueness of another. In other words, while Zizioulas accounts for the reality of human death, perhaps he could also account for the realities of human life.

Another possible shortcoming of Zizioulas' anthropology is his insistence that death prevents true personhood, and thus that only baptized Christians can truly be persons. As we have seen, because Zizioulas argues that since personhood "is created by the continuity of unbroken relationships," it is impossible for human beings to attain real personhood in this life. This introduces a tragic element into human life, since we will inevitably fall short of perfect relationality. Zizioulas' way out of this tragedy is to posit a kind of eschatological personhood that is accomplished through Baptism. The problem here, Edward Russell notes, is that "only certain people become persons when they experience salvation, participate in relationships at a certain level and are incorporated into the church." By suggesting that only unending relationships are truly constitutive of personhood and by insisting that only the 'new birth' of Baptism can enable these kinds of relationships, Zizioulas ultimately leaves us with the question of "whether or not there is personhood *extra ecclesia*."

Related to this problem is Zizioulas' understanding of death as something to be overcome. Zizioulas' understanding of death is that it is an inevitable, angst-inducing end to relationship and person, and a triumph of impersonal nature. What if we could imagine death otherwise? Beverly Clack has offered a feminist revisioning of death, challenging traditional notions of death as something to be overcome. She challenges the idea, which Zizioulas seems to hold to some extent, that "the ultimate transcendence of the physical world is believed to occur at death, when the soul escapes the prison of the body, and returns to the heavenly kingdom to share in the beatific vision." For many theologians and philosophers, including Zizioulas, death is something to be fought and ultimately overcome. We see this belief manifested in a variety of ways, from theologies of resurrection and promises of eternal life, to the quest for radical life extension from transhumanists. Life is often seen as an absolute good and death as something that can and ought to be overcome, or at least postponed. Clack, though, challenges this binary opposition of death and life and encourages a vision of mortality that places death in the midst of life. Seeing death only at the end of life, she argues, fails to acknowledge our limitations, such as sickness or injury, whereas placing death in the midst of life "enables us to see ourselves as part of the greater cosmic cycles of life, death, and renewal." Placing death in the midst of life, as Clack advocates, not only prevents us from thinking of death and life as binary terms, but also reminds us of our vulnerability; in trying to overcome death, we fight our vulnerability, but as we allow ourselves to become more comfortable with the cycles of life and death around us, we can become more comfortable with our vulnerability and finitude, which indeed "may lead to a deeper, more profound engagement with life, and with each other."

Could Zizioulas accept such an approach? Undoing the binary of death and life enables us to see death as a natural part of life rather than something to be overcome. This might minimize the importance of baptism and calls into question the basic Christian belief in life after death. This does not seem like a position that Zizioulas could accept, yet it could perhaps temper his reliance on ecclesiology to guarantee true human personhood. Clack's call to view death in the midst of life encourages Christians and non-Christians alike to become more aware of human vulnerability, and thus of the particularity and uniqueness of each person. While Zizioulas' relational anthropology relies on eternal, unbroken relationships to maintain personhood and he would not ultimately accept Clack's view, he might possibly appreciate her attention to how an awareness of vulnerability can encourage all humans to respect and love the uniqueness and fragility of those around them. Perhaps focusing on the vulnerabilities in the midst of life, both Christians and non-Christians could learn to become better persons.

LOOKING AHEAD

In this section we have seen the anthropological implications of Zizioulas' trinitarian theology. Zizioulas advocates a theology and an anthropology in which "to be and to be in relation become identical." Personal uniqueness is established in communion with others, and each person in this relational existence is unrepeatable and irreplaceable. In short, for Zizioulas, persons are absolutely unique and essentially relational and ought to be respected as such. Zizioulas' relational ontology and his attendant insistence on the absolute uniqueness of the person lead him to suggest an "ethical apophaticism." Persons are unclassifiable, and any attempt to ascribe a "positive qualitative content" to a person results in the loss of his or her uniqueness. For Zizioulas, we can only note "that someone simply is and is himself and not someone else." To say any more is to say too much; "a true ontology of personhood requires that the uniqueness of a person escape and transcend any qualitative kataphasis."

Zizioulas suggests "an *attitude*, an *ethos*" of communion and otherness, discouraging us from taking an objective and descriptive stance toward other people. Zizioulas' stance of "ethical apophaticism" respects the ontological uniqueness and relationality of the Other. In the next section, I further explore this notion of "ethical apophaticism." I first briefly show Zizioulas' understanding of this concept. I then introduce Luce Irigaray's concept of "wonder" as a similar idea. I use Irigaray's work both as a complement to Zizioulas' thought and as a way of pushing it farther. I also employ other ideas in Irigaray's work in the following chapters on Johnson and Keller, so that each of the three theologians has a common interlocutor. Finally, I suggest "wonder" as a virtue that emerges from Zizioulas' theology and is given sharper meaning from Irigaray's contributions.

Zizioulas, Ethics, and the Virtue of Wonder

"You, who are you? You who are not nor ever will be me or mine?"
-Luce Irigaray, *I Love to You*

In *Communion and Otherness*, Zizioulas suggests that his understanding of person is incompatible with any system of ethics as such. That our personhood is constituted by otherness, he argues, suggests not simply that we are different from each other, but that each of us is absolutely unique; "otherness, by definition, implies *uniqueness.*" As unique persons, then, we cannot be grouped or categorized. Thus Zizioulas argues that by "being a person, the Other is by definition unique and therefore unclassifiable. Only in this way can one remain truly and absolutely, that is, ontologically, Other." We cannot put people in boxes, nor can we group a number of persons under the category of "other;" each particular person we encounter is this "other," ontologically unique and defying categorization. It is for this reason, Zizioulas argues, that his understanding of personhood and systems of ethics are incompatible: "Otherness is a notion that, in its absolute sense, that is, in its truth, excludes generalizations of all kinds. Ethics, on the other hand, operates with general principles."

How, then, are we to proceed in the world? If, as Zizioulas insists, we cannot put persons, as uniquely other, into groups, what shape do our personal and communal lives take? Zizioulas does not leave us floundering. He argues not for a system of ethics as such, but rather for an ethos, a basic attitude that we have towards others whom we encounter: "communion and otherness are supposed to permeate and pervade our lives in their entirety. They are to become an *attitude*, an *ethos*, rather than an *ethic* and a set of principles." This ethos of otherness, or "ethical apophaticism," asks us to pause before each Other whom we encounter and let her disclose her uniqueness to us. When we begin to see each person as unique and unrepeatable, we begin to see each person as lovable.

Further, we are to love the Other not because of any of his specific moral qualities, or because he has lots of money, or because he is good looking. We are to love him simply because he is unique; "the Christian ethos of otherness does not allow for the acceptance or the rejection of the Other on the basis of his or her qualities, natural or moral. Everyone's otherness and uniqueness is to be respected on the simple basis of each person's ontological particularity and integrity." Here we see how Zizioulas' emphasis on personhood as ontological precludes us from judging others on their accidental qualities; "the more one loves ontologically and truly personally, the less dependent is such loving on the particular qualities of the person loved." Although Zizioulas rejects systems of ethics that operate with general principles, his "ethos of otherness" fits well in a virtue ethics framework. As we saw in the first chapter, virtues help us transition from who we are now to who we want to become. Zizioulas "ethos of otherness" or "ethical apophaticism," drawn from his understanding of persons (human and divine) as absolutely unique, encourages us to become respectful of difference and will train us to refrain from judging others on the basis of their external qualities. Below I offer a brief sketch of elements of Luce Irigaray's work that both complement and critique Zizioulas' understanding of "ethical apophaticism."

LUCE IRIGARAY'S CONTRIBUTIONS

Luce Irigaray was born in 1932 in Belgium. She holds doctorates in philosophy and linguistics, and she is also a practicing psychoanalyst. After her second doctoral thesis, *Speculum of the Other Woman*, in which she critiqued her mentor, Jacques Lacan, was published, she was ostracized from the French psychoanalytic community. She continued to write from a feminist perspective on a number of issues, and has since become a major voice in contemporary feminist theory, as well as being active in women's movements in France and Italy. In her work, she has engaged a broad range of thinkers, such as Plato, Aristotle, Plotinus, Renè Descartes, Immanuel Kant, G.W.F. Hegel, Sigmund Freud, Jacques Lacan, Karl Marx, Friedrich Nietzsche, Martin Heidegger, Jean-Paul Sartre, and Emmanuel Levinas, among others. Her work over the last 40 years has covered a good deal of territory, and some of it is notoriously difficult to understand. Among her interpreters, there is no consensus on the meaning of several of the major themes running through her work. All this is to say is that Irigaray's corpus is extensive and open to interpretation, and it is not my intention to cover it all here. Rather, I have chosen a few of her most salient ideas to put into conversation with themes in Zizioulas' work, and in later chapters, with the work of Elizabeth Johnson and Catherine Keller. With regard to Zizioulas, I focus primarily on her theme of wonder.

One major task of Irigaray's work is to think through new ways of relating to one another. Her early work focused on improving the relationship between men and women, since she believes that men's domination of women is the primary inequality and the cause of all other inequalities. Her later work both continues to emphasize the relationship between the sexes, as well as to expand to examine other relationships—between women, between men, between cultures, between humans and the earth, etc. Beginning with her work in the early 1980s and continuing in various ways today, Irigaray calls for relationships that are characterized by wonder. Drawing from Descartes' reflections on wonder, Irigaray suggests that this affection "beholds what it sees always as if for the first time, never taking hold of the other as its object. It does not try to seize, possess, or reduce this object, but leaves it subjective, still free." To wonder toward another person means to leave a space between yourself and the other and to let that person reveal him or herself to you. Ultimately this other is not completely knowable, and wonder, though it attracts me toward a person, also respects that interval between us.

For Irigaray, wonder happens primarily between two people of opposite sex. Although every other is unknowable to some extent, "the one who differs from me sexually" is forever and completely unknowable. We wonder most perfectly across the lines of sexual difference because women and men cannot be substituted for one another and thus are absolutely other. A woman will never be in a man's place nor a man in a woman's. This is not to say that wonder cannot happen between women or between men, but Irigaray insists on beginning with the relationships between men and women because, for her, these relationships are the source of the original inequality among humans.

Irigaray suggests that if wonder is to be our stance in the world, we must be "faithful to the perpetual newness of the self, the other, the world." The other ought to surprise us again and again as we learn not to impose our ideas of what he or she is or ought to be but rather "stop to look, at him or her, ask ourselves, come close to ourselves through questioning, *Who art thou?*" Thus wonder requires an epistemological humility in beholding the other.

Irigaray also touches on this theme of wonder in her later work, *I Love to You.* Here she replaces the phrase "I love you" with "I love *to* you," with the "to" meant as "the site of non-reduction of the person to the object." The "to" offers a linguistic space for the other and prevents appropriation of that other. Irigaray notes that to say "I love to you," rather than "I love you," encourages respect for the mystery of the other. Thus we see that "I love to you" complements her understanding of wonder, since each suggests that practicing relationships of non-appropriation, "which will enable us to respect ourselves and each other, form alliances, love ourselves and each other—as two or in the community—opens up the possibility for a fairer and better future."

Irigaray's use of wonder, her insistence on respect for the interval between two people, and her use of "I love to you" are similar to Zizioulas' ethos of communion and otherness; in each instance, the aim is to respect the uniqueness of the other and to refrain from describing or appropriating him or her. It is a call to "behold the unknown, to inhabit a new place, a place between 'me' and 'you' where we are confronted with the extraordinariness of each other."

For both Irigaray and Zizioulas, difference makes love and relationship possible. For Zizioulas, "the human being is *defined* through otherness. It is a being whose identity emerges only in relation to other beings." For Irigaray, "it takes two to love. To know how to separate and how to come back together," and how to respect the interval of difference between. Further, Irigaray's emphasis on correcting the relationships between men and women helps to highlight the importance of uncovering and eliminating relationships of inequality and domination. For Irigaray, this focus on the difference between the sexes is crucial to "living the relation between them differently" and is the beginning of enabling relationships of wonder between all people, regardless of gender.

THE VIRTUE OF WONDER

Thus far we have seen how Zizioulas' understanding of the Trinity leads to a certain understanding of humans and suggests a particular stance in the world. We have also seen how Irigaray's work complements Zizioulas' project. Based on the discussion so far, I suggest "wonder" as a virtue that emerges from Zizioulas' theology. The virtue of wonder is practiced in situations in which differences are seen to be threatening. I understand this virtue to have two moments: the first is similar to Zizioulas' "ethical apophaticism" and Irigaray's "I love to you" and consists in giving another person space to show him or herself and appreciating the goodness of him or her, without regard to external qualities. The second moment in the virtue of wonder, drawn loosely from Irigaray, consists in analyzing and/or deconstructing the categories, such as race, class, gender, sexuality, nationality, etc—that we use to define (and oftentimes oppress) others. (Though Irigaray argues that we should first address the relationships between men and women, I might suggest that the virtue of wonder can address any relationship.) Feminist theorist Mari Matsuda has proposed a method for uncovering the different forms of oppression and categorizing what might be at work in a particular situation. She calls this method, "ask the other question," and that is exactly how it works. If we are in a situation in which racism, for example, seems to be the predominant mode of subordination, we also ask, "Where is the sexism in this? Where is the patriarchy? Where are the class interests? Where is the heterosexism, and so on? These two moments of the virtue of wonder—a personal moment of leaving space and an analytic moment attending to the intersecting categories/oppressions at work—find their roots in Zizioulas' understanding of the absolute ontological uniqueness of the trinitarian persons and offer a way both to outgrow the fear of difference and to uncover ways in which differences have been exploited and used oppressively.

Applying the Virtue of Wonder

Miranda: "I understand Mr. Spock. The glory of creation is in its infinite diversity."

Spock: "And the ways our differences combine to create meaning and beauty."

--Star Trek Original Series, Season 3, Episode 5

The television shows and movies in the *Star Trek* franchise present a hopeful future vision of humanity, one in which, through technology, humans have eliminated disease and poverty and have come together as a species to explore the galaxy. Humans have taken to space to explore and "to seek out new life and new civilizations"—not to conquer or colonize, but to befriend and learn from. When encountering another life form, the members of Star Fleet show openness and respect, no matter how strange the aliens look or act. The crewmembers aboard the space stations and starships show no signs of superiority or revulsion at other life forms, but instead greet them with a desire to learn more about them. The characters on *Star Trek* consistently practice the virtue of wonder, never appropriating other cultures or individuals and always allowing newly encountered life forms to present themselves in their own way. The members of Star Fleet celebrate diversity and are not threatened by difference.

In the real world here and now, however, difference is a thornier issue. In the example below, I show how difference and communion can become complicated and how the virtue of wonder, particularly its attention to deconstructing and analyzing categories of difference, can be helpful. Every year since the integration of public schools in the 1960s, a few schools in a handful of counties in the deep south (primarily Georgia, Mississippi, and Alabama) have held segregated proms; there is a prom for the white students and a separate prom, on a separate day, for the black students. *The New York Times* highlighted one such school in 2009. Montgomery County High School, located in Montgomery County in south central Georgia, has had segregated proms since 1971, the first year the school was integrated. The comments made by the students interviewed in the article reveal mixed feelings. Most white students deny being racist and insist that they have black friends, yet they also argue that segregated proms are a tradition and make little effort to change it. The comments from the black students, on the other hand, are tinged with sadness and bitterness; "'I don't like segregated proms, there's no need for it...We went to school together and we all graduated at the same time. I feel like I've been deprived of something that was important to me,'" one student admits. Most of the students interviewed also suggest that it is the parents who push the hardest to keep the proms segregated. A white student claims that she was invited to the black prom, but that her mother would not allow her to go. How can Christian students and parents, white and black, practice the trinitarian virtue of wonder in this situation?

The first moment of wonder—leaving the space for another to express him or herself—seems to be partially at work already. For the most part, the students are friendly with each other and allow each other to be themselves. They argue that, most of the time, they do not see each other as black or white; the black and white students participate in clubs together, play sports together, and date each other. In this way, the students are learning to appreciate each other for who they are, without regard to race, the most obvious accidental quality at work in this example. It seems that the students and parents could most benefit from an exercise in the second moment of wonder, asking how they have failed to appreciate difference and how instead they have used difference in an oppressive way. Here it will be helpful to "ask the other question." Since race is the most obvious difference at work, we first ask, where is the racism? Racism could be at play in the very fact of the segregated prom, especially when we consider the offended attitudes of some of the black students. It is also evident in the fact that there are only two proms; which one do the Hispanic students attend, for example? The students, parents, and administrators are in a better position than I to reflect on other ways that racism functions, in the school, in families, and in the community. After an analysis of the racism at play, we then move on to the forms of difference that are in the background of this case: where is the sexism, classism, etc? The news article does not go into enough depth for me to be able to pursue these questions, but the virtue of wonder compels the students, administrators, and parents to raise and answer them, both individually and as a community. From this brief example, we can see that the virtue of wonder functions both as an immediate suspension of judgment of a person, and as a more extended reflection and conversation about the ways in which differences are used to oppress. At its heart, the virtue of wonder appreciates uniqueness and difference and the ways in which these can and should help form relationships of mutuality and respect.

Conclusion

John Zizioulas, drawing heavily on the Cappadocians, has given us an understanding of a triune God who exists as a communion of freely-given love between unique and irreplaceable persons. He shows, too, that human persons are likewise unique and essentially relational, but the problem of death is something that humans must overcome. Edward Russell suggests that "perhaps the greatest strength of Zizioulas' understanding of the person is his radically open-ended definition of the self as irreducible, uncontainable, and uncircumscribable, or rather, ecstatic and unique." Drawing from this notion of personhood and in dialogue with certain notions from Luce Irigaray's philosophy, I suggested "wonder" as the virtue implicit in Zizioulas' theology. The first moment of the virtue of wonder, drawn from Zizioulas' "ethical apophaticism" and Irigaray's "I love to you" is a moment of not judging accidental characteristics and "respecting you as other, accepting that I draw myself to a halt before you as before something insurmountable, a mystery." The second moment of wonder involves an examination and critique of the systems at work that have used difference to oppress.

We began with an image of God and moved from there to anthropology and virtues. I hope it is clear how both the anthropology and the virtue are implications of the theology. Zizioulas' image of divine persons as relational and unique, exchanging mutually-affirming gifts of love, has become one model for human relationships. In the next chapter, we will see another model of God, drawn from Elizabeth Johnson's work, which also suggests possibilities for the kinds of people we want to become.

4

The Theology of Elizabeth Johnson

"The bud
stands for all things,
even those things that don't flower,
for everything flowers, from within, of self-blessing;
though sometimes it is necessary
to reteach a thing its loveliness,
to put a hand on its brow
of the flower
and retell it in words and in touch
it is lovely
until it flowers again from within, of self-blessing..."

-Galway Kinnell, "St. Francis and the Sow"

In this chapter, I continue exploring the ways in which our images of God can affect how we understand ourselves and the kinds of virtues we wish to acquire. We move from John Zizioulas and the Christian East to the West, examining the work of Roman Catholic feminist theologian Elizabeth Johnson. Johnson is a religious sister in the Congregation of St Joseph and is currently a Distinguished Professor of Theology at Fordham University. Johnson has brought her feminist eye to a number of traditional Christian doctrines and figures, such as Mary, the communion of saints, Christology, and, of course, the Trinity. This chapter follows the same pattern as the last: I first examine Johnson's trinitarian theology through the lens of the four sources, then explore the anthropological implications of that theology, suggest a virtue, and offer an application of that virtue.

Elizabeth Johnson's Use of the Four Sources

Throughout most of her work, Johnson has turned to women's experiences as a vital source of theological knowledge. She has put these experiences into conversation with scripture and the Christian tradition to offer a feminist interpretation of classical doctrines. Her work on the Trinity follows such a method; drawing from women's experiences and recovering or reinterpreting images of God found in the scriptures and tradition, Johnson offers the symbol of She Who Is, a fully feminine image of God.

Johnson begins with Spirit-Sophia, who is God's personal engagement with and empowering presence in the world. Spirit-Sophia is everywhere, always drawing near and passing by, providing a healing and encouraging presence in a conflictual world. Next comes Jesus-Sophia, whose humiliating death on a cross overturns patriarchal understandings of masculinity. What Jesus-Sophia represents is not exclusion or domination or maleness, but "otherness that freely draws near, bringing new life, sustaining all loves." Finally, Johnson turns to Mother-Sophia, the creative, life-giving force of all that exists. The metaphor of mother, she argues, is associated with our early experiences of comfort, play, discovery, nurture, love, and security. The metaphor of mother also suggests a close relationship between God and the world, as if we are all enfolded in Her womb. Whereas the image of "Father" has become literalized and can serve to perpetuate patriarchy, Johnson argues, the image of God as Mother opens up fresh ways of understanding God's compassionate, creative power.

In the pages that follow, we will further explore Johnson's symbol of She Who Is and the sources she has relied upon to construct it. We turn first to Johnson's use of experience as a source for theological knowledge.

EXPERIENCE

Whereas John Zizioulas engages the Christian tradition as his primary source of theological knowledge, Elizabeth Johnson begins with "a source that has been almost totally neglected by traditional theology—the experience of women, especially poor women." Below I focus on two ways in which Johnson draws from women's experience —women's experiences of conversion and women's experiences of suffering—in constructing her model of God.

First, Johnson examines women's experiences of conversion from oppression to liberation. She notes two aspects of this conversion: contrast and confirmation. First, women's experiences of suffering contrast with their sense of dignity and their own humanity. Having felt various forms of oppression, Johnson argues, women (or any oppressed persons) grow indignant, and "the judgment arises: we are worth more than this." The contrast between the experience of oppression and the sense of one's own dignity challenges one to address and confront the sources of the oppression.

The second aspect of women's conversion that Johnson notes is confirmation, a positive acknowledgement of women's worth through memory, narrative, and solidarity. While the moment of contrast makes women aware of their oppression, the moment of confirmation affirms, through narrative remembrance, what women sense in the contrast—that they are "not non-persons or half persons or deficient persons, but genuine subjects of history."

Women's "no" to subjection and "yes" to their own worth is based in their experiences and enables conversion. Johnson notes that her understanding of "conversion" differs from its traditional usage. Traditionally, she argues, conversion has been understood as a process of disowning oneself or making oneself lesser and God greater. Because women have historically been relegated to the margins as the "lesser sex," this type of conversion would be harmful to women rather than spiritually enriching. Johnson argues that the type of conversion women are called to undergo is not conversion as loss of self but rather conversion as "discovery of self and affirmation of one's strength, giftedness, and responsibility...turning away from demeaning female identity toward new ownership of the female self as God's good gift." Thus, based on women's experiences of oppression, Johnson redefines conversion as self-affirmation rather than self-abnegation.

Johnson further argues that women's experiences of conversion entail new ways of understanding God. She argues that women's conversion to self-affirmation calls in turn for the theological affirmation that women are created in the image of God and bear the image of Christ. In order to give theological affirmation to women's conversion, Johnson offers an understanding of the Trinity in feminine terms. Not satisfied with attempts to describe a few feminine characteristics in a generally masculine God, to pose the Holy Spirit as the 'female' member of the Trinity, or to switch paradigms to an earth-goddess, Johnson offers an understanding of the Trinity—She Who Is—as a fully feminine alternative to the dominant masculine model. The traditional formulation—Father, Son, and Holy Spirit—she argues, has become literalized, hegemonic, and too closely associates God with maleness; this symbol excludes women from claiming full ownership of their identity as *imago Dei.* Johnson's symbol of She Who Is, drawn in part from women's experiences of conversion, aims to recover the dignity of women as created in the image of God; "the changing history of women's self appraisal and self-naming creates a new situation for language about divine mystery."

In constructing her theology, Johnson draws not only from women's conversion experiences and self-affirmation but also from their experiences of suffering. She explores women's experiences of giving birth, anger, grief, and degradation as possible starting points for language about God. She notes that women's experiences of giving birth can offer us language for God that evokes an image of God crying out in labor, "pushing with all her might to bring forth justice, the fruit of her love." The intense suffering and creative power of giving birth emphasizes the depth of God's involvement in the world. Johnson also draws from women's experiences of anger to offer language for God. She notes that, "when women awaken to the ravages wreaked upon them and those they love by unjust patriarchal systems, they typically get angry." This anger, she notes, drawing from Beverly Harrison's work, reveals that something is amiss in our relationships and serves as a call to action and resistance. Johnson notes that women's experiences of anger about the injustices they and others have suffered can give rise to a powerful image of God's own righteous anger, which she interprets as a mode of caring response in the face of evil. This image of God "stands as an antidote to sentimentality in our view of God's holy mystery as love, and as a legitimation of women's anger at the injustice of their own diminishment and the violation of those they love."

A third experience of suffering that Johnson draws from is women's grief at the suffering of those they love. This evokes an image of God's own grief at the suffering of Her creation; the symbol of a grieving God works to console those who are suffering by revealing God's compassionate presence in the midst of that suffering. As Johnson puts it, "weeping women, women whose hearts moan like a flute because those they love have come to harm, are everywhere in the world. As *imago Dei* they point to the mystery of divine sorrow, of an unimaginable compassionate God who suffers with beloved creation. Holy Wisdom keeps vigil through endless hours of pain while her grief awakens protest."

A final experience of suffering Johnson draws from is degradation, the most terrible kind of experience, felt most keenly in rape, beatings, and other kinds of sexual abuse. Calling to mind the broken and beaten bodies of women, Johnson suggests that "in an unspeakable way they are images of the crucified." Drawing images of God from these experiences enables us to see God's participation in the suffering of the world most intensely.

Johnson argues these four experiences of women's suffering—giving birth, anger, grief, and degradation—can offer language for God that makes God more accessible in times of disaster or despair. She notes that the traditional understanding of God as impassible, or beyond suffering, can lead to understandings of God as removed or uncaring. Drawing from women's experiences of suffering when choosing our language for God, on the other hand, gives rise to understandings of God as compassionately present with us in our suffering. By taking seriously women's experiences of and responses to suffering, Johnson notes, we begin to see that "the idea that God might permit great suffering while at the same time remaining unaffected by the distress of beloved creatures is not seriously imaginable."

As we have just seen, Johnson values women's experience as an important, but overlooked, source of theological knowledge. By attending to women's experiences of conversion to self-affirmation, she argues that a conversion of our images of God must follow in order to reflect more fully women's understanding of themselves as created in the image of God. By attending to women's experiences of suffering, Johnson offers images of God as compassionate and present with us in our suffering. While Johnson's primary source of theological knowledge is perhaps these experiences of women, she engages other sources as well, as we will see in the following sections.

TRADITION

Johnson employs experience as the most significant source of theological knowledge, yet she is careful also to engage tradition and scripture in her work. I turn now to her use of tradition, from which she draws widely but selectively. Johnson engages the Christian tradition both at a general epistemological level and in constructing her particular interpretation of God. First, she borrows three traditional concepts that deal with the possibilities and limits of speaking about and knowing God. The first of these concepts is divine incomprehensibility. Citing theologians from Clement of Alexandria to Thomas Aquinas to Karl Rahner, Johnson argues that the tradition has consistently held that God is ultimately unknowable and indescribable—a mystery, in other words. Because of this doctrine of divine incomprehensibility or hiddenness, all of our language about God will fall short, and no single symbol will suffice. Johnson argues that this traditional understanding of God's unknowability gives credence to the feminist effort to include many metaphors for God; feminine, masculine and, non-human metaphors for God are equally "legitimate and inadequate" expressions of "what is ultimately inexpressible."

Related to the inability of human language to give adequate expression to the divine mystery is the second aspect of the tradition from which Johnson draws—analogy. The words we use to describe God are meant not literally but analogically. Drawing again from Thomas Aquinas, Johnson notes that our analogical talk of God involves a threefold movement of affirmation, negation, and eminence. In the first move, a term we use for humans (such as "good") is affirmed of God (God is good). In the second move, that term is negated to remove it from creaturely ways of being (God is not good in the way humans are good). In the third move, the term "is predicated of God in a supereminent way that transcends all cognitive capabilities" (God is good not as humans are good, but in a more excellent way as the source of all good). This understanding of speech about God as analogical, Johnson argues, can serve as a critique of patriarchal understandings of God; that our masculine analogies for God still tend to give us a sense of God as male indicates that these analogies have not been sufficiently negated. One task of feminist theology, then, is to continue to insist upon the analogical nature of all language for God.

A final insight from the Christian tradition from which Johnson draws is the need for many names for God. This flows again from God's incomprehensibility; none of our names for God are completely adequate, so the more names we use the better able we are to get at different aspects of God's nature. Drawing from Thomas Aquinas, post-biblical Jewish literature, and African theologians, Johnson shows that using many names for God has been a consistent practice of the Christian tradition. Johnson also notes that these elements of the tradition she has emphasized are often overlooked:

In spite of the tradition's insistence on the radical incomprehensibility of God; in spite of the teaching that all words for God, being finite, fall short of their intended goal; and in spite of the presence of many names, images, and concepts for the divine in the Scripture and later Christian tradition, this tradition has lifted up the patriarchal way of being human to functional equivalence with the divine.

Johnson thus argues for renewed attention to those aspects of tradition that have been neglected in order that our images of God become once again worthy reflections both of human experience and of God's own nature.

In addition to these three traditional insights—divine incomprehensibility, analogy, and many names—Johnson also draws from specific aspects of the tradition in constructing her model of God as She Who Is. In her discussion of Spirit-Sophia, for example, Johnson traces the development of the theology of the Holy Spirit and shows that, for most of the church's history, the Spirit has taken a back seat to the Father and the Son. She notes that in many patristic texts the Spirit is dealt with last, almost as an afterthought and that post-reformation Catholicism institutionalized the Spirit, "tying the Spirit's activity very tightly to ecclesiastical office and ordained ministry...thus ensuring that the radical freedom of the Spirit is controlled by subordination to ecclesiastical order and discipline." Yet Johnson also finds glimmers of hope in the tradition and uses these to help construct her own theology of the Holy Spirit. She draws, for example, on Thomas Aquinas' understanding of the Spirit as love and gift.

Johnson also argues for a recovery of a strong theology of the Spirit, noting that, although this person of the Trinity has traditionally been overshadowed by the Father and the Son, the Spirit is actually the most immanent and present member of the Trinity. In her lecture, "Women, Earth, and Creator Spirit," for example, Johnson calls for renewed attention to the Spirit. She notes that humans have three basic relationships—with one another, with the earth, and with God. In each of these, she argues, the female element has been disparaged. Thus, men have tended to dominate women in human relationships, God tends to be associated with masculine qualities and given masculine names, and the earth, often associated with women and fertility, has been left open to misuse and destruction. Placing more emphasis on the Spirit, Johnson argues, can begin to heal each of these relationships, especially our relationship with the earth. Recognizing the Spirit's continual presence in and involvement with the world, Johnson argues that "the Spirit is life who gives life...moving over the world, breathing into the chaos, pouring out, informing, quickening, warming, setting free, blessing, dancing in mutual immanence with the world." Johnson challenges the traditional marginalization of the Spirit, arguing that the Spirit enfolds and sustains the world as a powerful and creative force.

Johnson also draws from tradition in her discussion of Jesus-Sophia and Mother-Sophia. Her attitude towards traditional Christology is largely negative, and she notes that "the powerful symbol of the liberating Christ lost its subversive, redemptive significance" as Jesus came to be seen as King or Lord and when his maleness came to be seen as essential to his identity. Most of Johnson's work on Jesus is an effort to overturn patriarchal images of Jesus in favor of a Christology that emphasizes mutuality, comfort, and challenge, as we will see in the next section. Johnson also notes that the tradition has neglected images of God as Mother, pointing to a long history of the subordination and devaluation of women. She singles out Thomas' anthropology, which understands women to be defective and passive, but Thomas is by no means the only or the worst offender; in a tradition spanning at least from Aristotle to modern teachings of the Roman Catholic church, Johnson notes, women have been consistently undervalued, maligned, and abused, both in theological writings and in their everyday lives. Given this long tradition of a dualistic anthropology, Johnson argues, it is understandable that the image of God as Mother would have been neglected or rejected. Thus her emphasis on women's experience; when women begin to reflect on their experiences, both their experiences of their goodness and their suffering, new images of God, such as Mother, become possible.

As we have seen, Johnson turns to tradition to support the theological knowledge gained by attending to women's experiences. She engages aspects of the tradition that have been forgotten, such as the imperative to use many names for God, as well as those aspects in need of feminist reinterpretation. In so doing, she is able to offer fresh readings of each person of the Trinity. In short, Johnson "risks new interpretations of the tradition in conversation with women's lives." Johnson also notes the shadow of patriarchy looming over the tradition, which has contributed to the lack of feminine imagery for God, the elevation of Jesus' masculinity, and the devaluation of the Spirit, women, and the earth.

SCRIPTURE

Just as Johnson is careful to draw from and critique traditional sources in constructing her theology, so too does she both critique aspects of scripture and turn to other aspects of it to support the images of God she has chosen. Drawing from the documents of Vatican II, Johnson argues that not all aspects of scripture are inerrant, such as those that contain inaccurate historical or scientific information. Instead, she offers a principle of interpretation that holds that scripture is inerrant in matters that concern our salvation; "the Bible was not written to teach the natural sciences nor to give information about political history, but to witness to God's graciousness in the midst of a broken world." Joining her feminist perspective with this principle of interpretation, Johnson argues that those aspects or interpretations of scripture that diminish the image of God in women or legitimate their subordination are not salvific. She then turns to a number of images of God in the scriptures that can be interpreted as salvific from a feminist perspective.

Johnson first notes Jesus' use of *abba* ("Father ") to name God. She notes that some interpreters take Jesus' use of this paternal name to be exclusive in such a way that Christians today are only authorized to call God "Father." Johnson, on the other hand, calls into question both the frequency and the exclusivity of Jesus' use of *abba*. Drawing from the parables, she notes that Jesus' language about God is actually varied and colorful, employing such images as a woman searching for a lost coin, a shepherd looking for lost sheep, or a wind that blows where it wills. She also notes that, while it is probable that Jesus did use *abba* to refer to God, this usage is not so frequent as some Christians believe. The term appears only four times in Mark, the first Gospel written, and increases in each subsequently written Gospel to 15 times in Luke, 49 in Matthew, and 109 in John, suggesting that the use of the term "Father" became increasingly important in early Christian communities, as "a subtle endorsement of the priority of the father in social arrangements," but that it might not have been so central to Jesus himself. Johnson further notes that when Jesus does use *abba*, the term connotes not a patriarchal figure but a compassionate and intimate one.

In addition to Jesus' use of *abba*, Johnson also explores scriptural uses of spirit, wisdom, and mother as symbols of God that can be interpreted as liberating and salvific for women. First, pointing to the Psalms, as well as to Genesis, Exodus, Isaiah, Luke, and John, Johnson argues that the image of God as Spirit is prevalent throughout scripture, noting that the Spirit's activities are often "feminine:" creating new life, grieving over destruction, hovering like a nesting mother bird or sheltering her people under the shadow of her wings. The image of God as Spirit, then, is one that can be liberating for women and one with which their experiences may resonate.

The same can be said of Wisdom, or *Sophia*, Johnson argues; "the biblical depiction of Wisdom is itself consistently female, casting her as sister, mother, female beloved, chef and hostess, preacher, judge, liberator, establisher of justice, and a myriad of other female roles wherein she symbolizes transcendent power ordering and delighting in the world." Wisdom appears briefly in Job and Baruch and prominently in the books of Proverbs, Sirach, the and Wisdom of Solomon. Johnson notes that while the appearance of Wisdom in each of these books is different, one possible interpretation that is consistent with each of the books is that Wisdom is a female personification of God's own being; "She is all-knowing, all-powerful, and present everywhere, renewing all things. Active in creation, she also works in history to save her chosen people, guiding and protecting them through the vicissitudes of struggle." This interpretation, grounded in scripture, of *Sophia* as the female personification of God is one major factor that enables Johnson to construct her trinitarian theology in feminine terms; each person of the Trinity is re-interpreted through Sophia so that they "cohere with women's experience of the holy and press toward renewed speech about the mystery of God."

Johnson's interpretations of the scriptural uses of *Sophia* and *abba* have been questioned by some biblical scholars. Mary Rose D'Angelo, for example, has encouraged Johnson to acknowledge the patriarchal contexts of the biblical wisdom traditions from which she draws and argues that Johnson has drawn only from one strand of scriptural images of *Sophia*. D'Angelo also suggests, against Johnson, that Jesus' use of *abba* is patriarchal, but in a way that is characterized by justice. In a brief essay, Johnson has responded to these critiques. She argues that she chose to emphasize the personal function of *Sophia* because it is the one that gives Her divine status unequivocally. The other appearances of *Sophia,* she suggests, can be interpreted as something less than God. She further notes that she will give more thought to the ways in which other scriptural instantiations of Sophia may be sources for emancipatory speech about God. As for D'Angelo's understanding of Jesus' use of *abba,* Johnson argues that "patriarchy and justice are contradictory stances" and continues to hold that *abba* did not invoke a patriarchal God. As Johnson explains her interpretations of scripture, she acknowledges that she herself is not a biblical scholar and that she always appreciates input from those whose area of expertise is scripture. She graciously defends her own positions while remaining open to new insights or suggestions.

As with her engagement with tradition, Johnson aims to recover overlooked aspects of scripture, such as *Sophia,* and to reinterpret other aspects from a feminist liberation perspective, such as Jesus' use of *abba.* In short, Johnson interprets scripture through the lens of women's experiences to support a liberatory and affirmative vision of God.

SECULAR DISCIPLINES OF KNOWLEDGE

The main focus of much of Johnson's theological work has been her exploration of how women's experiences complement or critique aspects of scripture and the Christian tradition. Of the four sources, she is the least explicit about her use of secular disciplines of knowledge. In *She Who Is,* for example, she has chapters on scripture, tradition, and experience, but not on secular disciplines of knowledge. Though she does not employ secular disciplines as explicitly as the other sources, she does engage sources such as feminist theory and the physical sciences throughout her work.

For example, in her discussion of God as Mother, Johnson draws from feminist theorists such as Adrienne Rich and Carol Gilligan to uncover and reject patriarchal constructions of motherhood. Though Johnson does not often explicitly employ secular feminist theory, her work is nonetheless shaped by it. She draws from numerous feminist theologians, whose own work has been shaped in various ways by feminist theory, and she is sensitive to common feminist concerns such as essentialism, relationality, difference, and the interlocking oppressions of race, class, gender, sexuality, etc.

In her more recent *Quest for the Living God*, Johnson engages the physical sciences. For example, she draws from evolutionary theory and quantum physics to develop a more panentheistic account of the Spirit. Panentheism, as Johnson understands it, is an alternative to both pantheism, in which God is everything, and theism, in which God is completely separate from the world. In contrast to both of these positions, panentheism posits that God is *in* all; unlike pantheism, which collapses the distinction between God and the world or theism, which insists on their absolute difference, panentheism offers a vision of God intimately involved in the world, compassionately encompassing and sustaining all things. Johnson shows how contemporary evolutionary theory complements this understanding of God by offering an interpretation of the Spirit as a wellspring of novelty, setting the universe off on a grand adventure and displaying an openness to the future; "throughout the vast sweep of cosmic and biological evolution, the Spirit embraces the material root of life and its endless new potential, empowering the cosmic process from within."

Johnson also emphasizes the element of chance. She argues that the Enlightenment God of order is no longer tenable given the contributions of modern science. She notes the "uncertainty principle" of quantum physics, which describes our inability to determine both the speed and the position of a single particle at a given time, and the theory of natural selection as an open-ended and unpredictable process of adaptation, as two examples of the role of uncertainty and chance in modern science. Given these and other examples of scientific advances, Johnson concludes that "as boundless love at work in the ongoing evolution of the universe, divine creativity is the source not just of cosmic order but also of the chance that allows novelty to appear."

Johnson's use of the secular disciplines is implicit, but pervasive. She shows a willingness to engage with outside disciplines and to reconsider theological positions in light of developments in these disciplines. Still, women's experiences tend to be the driving force; the secular disciplines Johnson engages favor her interpretation of women's experience and help promote a vision of the triune God that is liberatory for women. Nonetheless, Johnson does show a clear openness to the role outside disciplines can play in shaping our understandings of God.

FEMINIST READINGS OF JOHNSON'S USE OF THE FOUR SOURCES

Though Johnson writes from a feminist perspective, aspects of her theology are open to criticism from other feminist perspectives. The ways in which Johnson draws from tradition, for example, could draw criticism; some feminists have rejected the Christian tradition as inherently and irredeemably patriarchal. Of these "radical" thinkers, Mary Daly is perhaps the most notorious. Daly challenged Christian feminists to find the "Courage to Leave," which she defines as the "virtue enabling women to depart from all patriarchal religions and other hopeless institutions; resolution springing from deep knowledge of the nucleus of nothingness which is at the core of these institutions." Daly and other thinkers who have determined the Christian tradition to be oppressive would take issue with Johnson's continued use of it.

Johnson falls into a group of "reformers" in feminist Christian theology who, though noting the pervasive patriarchal bias of the tradition, nonetheless insist that the core of the tradition is liberating rather than oppressive. In this respect, Johnson's engagement with the tradition can be held as a model. She draws widely from the whole history of Christian thought to uncover both methodological approaches and symbols that can foster the emancipation of women towards full flourishing.

Mary McClintock Fulkerson has also challenged Johnson to push her thinking further in certain areas. First, Fulkerson asks whether Johnson's symbol of She Who Is really moves beyond gender binaries.

She agrees with Johnson's rejection of "add-a-trait" images of God, which pose a masculine and complementary feminine side to the persons of the Trinity because this supports a binary based on stereotypical gendered traits. Fulkerson notes that Johnson aims for "transformation of an oppressive system, not simply an inclusion of women in it," but she wonders if Johnson's She Who Is simply moves beyond the subordination of the feminine to create a binary of competing equals. Though Johnson argues that she does not intend for any single symbol of God, even She Who Is, to be used exclusively, Fulkerson contends that "the reduction in most Christian communities of the trinity to the Father-Son-Holy Spirit formula has virtually eliminated the more evocative broader semantic field before; it could happen again" with a fully feminine symbol. She thus pushes Johnson to move even further beyond gender binaries by drawing images of God not just from women's experiences, but from the experiences of gay, lesbian, transgender, and intersex persons. Fulkerson notes that Johnson's Jesus-Sophia already contains seeds of such an exploration. She asks Johnson to speak to the transsexual implications of saying that the man Jesus is indwelt by a She (*Sophia*).

A second critique Fulkerson offers has to do with Johnson's treatment of the differences among women, particularly the impact of race and class on women's experiences. Fulkerson notes that Johnson intends the broadest sense of "women" and that, for the most part, she succeeds in employing this broad category while also remaining sensitive to the vast differences among the women of the world. Fulkerson does, however, encourage Johnson to consider how symbols may work differently in different social locations and to ask "not simply whether we redress the dominance of male imagery with female imagery, but the larger one about the complexity of the relationship between social location and theological and gender differences." In other words, Fulkerson challenges Johnson to more carefully consider how the symbol of God might function differently from culture to culture and the ways in which different cultures produce and maintain those symbols.

Other feminist theologians may also question Johnson's understanding of women's experience. Serene Jones has offered a typology of the ways in which feminist theologians understand "women's experience." This typology has two major positions—1) essentializing accounts of women's experience, drawn from phenomenology, process theology, or literary analysis, and 2) accounts of women's experience that emphasize "the historical and cultural texture of identity and language," drawn from either cultural anthropology or poststructuralism. Because each of these ends of the typology has its own unique shortcomings, Jones dubs the first position the "rock" and the second the "hard place;" interpreting women's experiences thus puts one between a rock and a hard place.

Jones puts Johnson's understanding of women's experience in the "rock," that is, among those accounts of experience that tend to be essentializing. Like Fulkerson, Jones notes that Johnson offers a structurally universal account of experience and language and does not take well enough into account the ways in which symbols and experiences are shaped by culture. The positive aspects of Johnson's work, Jones argues, are that it is able to give a generalized account of human experience and is thus able to offer images of God that are, presumably, accessible in one way or another to all people, and, further, that it is "written in a language which invites the reader into an inclusive and hope-filled textual drama where God and the creature meet in an empowering embrace." The downside, however, to Johnson's approach is its "resistance to racially historicizing identity, its idealist tendency toward expressive symbolism, and its potentially reductive drive to generate exhaustive accounts of experiential structures." In other words, as Jones sees it, Johnson is able to give a generalized account of women's experience that leads to compelling images of God, but often does so to the exclusion of the effects of race, class, and other sites of difference on how one might shape and perceive symbols of God.

The flip side of Jones' typology, the "hard place," has almost the opposite problem; by attending carefully to sites of difference and particularity, these interpretations of experience often fail to give a useful account of experience that can be used generally. Jones encourages all feminist theologians, including Johnson, to occupy the tight space between the "rock" and the "hard place," trying to balance giving a general account of experience with taking seriously the very real impacts of race, class, and other differences on women's experience.

In addition to critiques from other feminist theologians, Johnson has also drawn critique from explicitly non-feminist Christian theologians. R.R. Reno, for one, takes issue with Johnson's engagement with tradition. He argues that, for Johnson and other feminist theologians, the Christian tradition is subordinated to a feminist ethical vision, and whatever does not fit with this ethical vision is rejected. Up to this point Johnson would probably agree; for her, the critical principle of interpretation is women's flourishing, and aspects of scripture or tradition that thwart this flourishing are not to be trusted; "Christian feminist liberation theology is reflection on religious mystery from a stance which makes an a priori option for the human flourishing of women."

Reno, however, interprets such a move as entirely selfish, arguing that "the anchor becomes oneself" rather than the wisdom of the inherited tradition. Thus, for him, Johnson's project is ultimately one of self-love, which he interprets negatively as a selfish and hostile attitude toward tradition. Here the tension between women's experience and the tradition comes to the fore. Whereas Reno argues that Johnson has cast aside much of the tradition "as unusable detritus," Johnson would argue that her critical feminist principle serves not only to liberate women but also to liberate the tradition itself. Further, Johnson would take issue with Reno's negative understanding of self-love. For her, bringing women's experience, especially women's conversion to self-affirmation, to bear on aspects of the tradition is a positive act of self-love. Women affirm their experiences and claim themselves as made in the image of God. This act of self-love is liberating not just for women, but for all Christians and for our understandings of God.

LOOKING FORWARD

In this section, we have seen how Johnson engages the four sources of experience, tradition, scripture, and secular disciplines in her trinitarian theology. Both drawing from and critiquing aspects of scripture and tradition, she has offered Spirit-Sophia, Jesus-Sophia, and Mother-Sophia—She Who Is—as a liberative symbol of God. Perhaps her most important point is that women's experiences can tell us something about God. She thus takes women's experiences as a legitimate and valuable source of theological knowledge, interpreting scripture and tradition in light of these experiences. The result, as we have seen, is the both liberation of women and of patriarchalized images of God. In the next section, I explore some of the anthropological implications of this liberating She Who Is.

Anthropological Implications of Johnson's Theology

"However, the majority of women are neither harlots nor courtesans; nor do they sit clasping pug dogs to dusty velvet all through the summer afternoon."

-Virginia Woolf, A Room of One's Own

Johnson's trinitarian theology has a number of implications for how we understand ourselves. In this section I explore several of these: her understanding of women as imago Dei and as imago Christi; her emphasis on trinitarian mutuality, equality, and diversity; and her emphasis on using many names for God.

First, Johnson's symbol of She Who Is emphasizes that women are created in the image of God and in the image of Christ. By offering a fully feminine understanding of the Trinity, Johnson encourages women to claim their dignity as made in the image of God; "the wholeness of women's reality is affirmed as created by God and blessed with the identity of being in the divine images and likeness." Johnson's fully feminine symbol of God affirms women's experiences, lives, and their very personhood. Johnson argues that this symbol of She Who Is empowers women to address the suffering in the world:

What is modeled in this language is the exuberant dignity and life-giving power of women, for here divine mystery, darkly known through creation, salvation, and the ongoing dialectic of presence and absence, appears in female gestalt, and divine blessing comes as a female gift. Such a symbol of God signifies for women the call to grow into the abundance of their human powers, to be creative, self-expressive, and loving together in ways that address human brokenness, violence, and the destruction of the earth.

By encouraging and empowering women to see the image of God in themselves, Johnson's trinitarian theology calls not simply for women's self-affirmation (a very important move in itself) but also for women to enter into compassionate and creative relationship with others and with the earth.

Further, Johnson's feminist interpretation of Jesus-Sophia insists that women are not only in the image of God but also in the image of Christ, a point which comes to bear on debates about women's ordination in the Roman Catholic church, as we will see in the final section of this chapter. For Johnson, Jesus' maleness is an accidental characteristic of his humanity, and does not exclude women from ministry or justify their subordination in any way. Instead, in Jesus we see "Sophia herself personally pitching her tent in the flesh of humanity to teach the paths of justice." Thus, as both women and men, lay and ordained, come to see themselves not only in the image of God but also in the image of Christ, the call to practice compassion and justice becomes clearer. Jesus embodies—incarnates—Sophia's compassionate and life-giving solidarity with human beings; as humans conformed to the image of Christ, we are called to also embody such characteristics.

Johnson's trinitarian theology has further anthropological implications in its emphasis on mutual relation, radical equality, and community in diversity as central characteristics of God. Johnson offers friendship as a metaphor for the kind of relationality within the Trinity, noting that friendship is the most mutual of relationships. Johnson's emphasis on experience allows experience and our images of God to be mutually enriching; our experiences of friendship tell us something about God, and in turn, understanding God as friend enhances our understanding of human friendship. Understanding God's relationality in terms of mutuality and friendship serves as a critique of those forms of human relationality that privilege hierarchy or domination; "the eternal friendship that is the triune mystery of Sophia opens to encompass the whole broken world through awakening friends of God to the praxis of compassion and freedom."

In addition to mutual relation, Johnson also emphasizes radical equality as a trinitarian characteristic. Johnson argues that the symbol of the Trinity reflects a community of equals in which "there is no subordination, no before or after, no first, second, and third, no dominant and marginalized." This, in turn, offers a vision of human equality.

Finally, Johnson emphasizes community in diversity as another essential characteristic of the Trinity, suggesting that divine unity must be understood as inter-relational. She offers the Greek term *perichoresis*, which is related to the term for a circle dance and signifies a cyclical, rhythmic movement, as one way of understanding the unity in diversity of the Trinity. Each trinitarian person encompasses and moves in and around the others in "a clasping of hands, a pervading exchange of life, a genuine circling around together that constitutes the permanent, active, divine *koinonia*." The perichoretic movements of the persons of the Trinity also offer insight into human community. *Perichoresis* involves freedom of movement and expression, coupled with an awareness of the movements and expressions of others. In other words, as human persons, we are all involved in this perichoretic dance of life, called to move as unique individuals in coordinated and graceful ways with others.

Johnson's emphasis on trinitarian mutuality, equality, and community in diversity offer powerful anthropological implications, critiquing self-centeredness and all forms of domination. The Trinity, as Johnson understands it, "provides a symbolic picture of totally shared life at the heart of the universe...Mutual relationship of different equals appears as the ultimate paradigm of personal and social life."

Another aspect of Johnson's work with anthropological implications is her insistence on using multiple names and metaphors for God. Here again human experience and language for God are mutually informative; the experience of many ways of being human leads to many images of God, which in turn reinforces an openness to different ways of being human. Johnson has focused on gender, essentially arguing that being a woman is a legitimate way of being human, but the argument can be extended to other oppressed or marginalized groups. Johnson's insistence on employing many images of God shows that the patriarchal understanding of God is not the only one. When we use many images of God, we begin to see the many ways that humans can reflect the image of God in themselves.

Johnson's symbol of God encourages self-affirmation, just, mutual, and compassionate relationships, and an openness to different ways of being human. Her mothering, nurturing, ever-present God reminds us that we have come forth from God and that we daily depend on God's grace and compassion. That She Who Is birthed the whole universe reminds us of our kinship with the earth and all of its creatures; we owe respect not only to each other, but also to every other created thing, born as we are of the same God. Finally, her symbol of She Who Is reminds us that all of us—male and female—are equal in our dignity as creatures made in the image of God. In her own words, "only a community of equals related in profound mutuality, only a community pouring itself out for justice, peace, and the integrity of creation, corresponds to the triune symbol."

Johnson's Theology and the Virtue of Self-Esteem

"Women name themselves as subjects of authentic and full humanity."

-Rosemary Radford Ruether, *Sexism and God Talk*

Elizabeth Johnson's trinitarian theology draws from women's experiences, both positive and negative, and, in conversation with tradition and scripture, offers a fully feminine symbol of God while also encouraging the use of multiple images of God. Because, for Johnson, "the symbol of God functions" as the ultimate reference point for how we understand the world and ourselves, a fully feminine symbol encourages women to see in themselves the image of God. Johnson's symbol of She Who Is, I argue, encourages the virtue of self-esteem. Because self-esteem is a term that is open to multiple interpretations, as I define it I engage not only the work of Luce Irigaray, as I do in other chapters, but also the works of two the Christian virtue theorists we saw in Chapter One—Paul Wadell and James Keenan—who offer virtues that are similar to self-esteem. In this conversation between Irigaray, Wadell, Keenan, and Johnson herself, my own understanding of self-esteem should become clear. I first note the relevant contributions of each of these thinkers, beginning with Johnson, and then offer a definition of the virtue of self-esteem.

The most salient aspects of Johnson's theology that come to bear on the virtue of self-esteem are her emphasis on conversion, the promotion of women's full humanity, and the symbol of She Who Is. As we saw earlier, Johnson understands conversion as a process of contrast and confirmation that leads to self-affirmation and a rejection of the oppression one has experienced. Further, Johnson insists on taking "the total personhood of women with utter seriousness." Taking the full humanity of women seriously requires care for women's emotional, physical, and spiritual lives as well as their personal and social relationships. Promoting the total personhood of women means promoting every aspect of women's lives. Finally, the symbol of She Who Is serves as an empowering and liberating divine image for women. This symbol emphasizes women as created in the image of God, affirming women's conversion experiences to self-affirmation. Ultimately, She Who Is "is the dark radiance of love in solidarity with the struggle of denigrated persons, including long generations of women, to shuck off their mean estate and lay hold of their genuine human dignity and value."

Luce Irigaray, like Johnson, challenges the exclusively male language of the traditional trinitarian formulation. In the symbol of the Trinity, women are excluded, and an all-male God is "not enough to sanctify the female sex." Underlying Irigaray's critique of Western theology is her sense that it is necessary to have an image of the divine as a horizon for human becoming. For Irigaray, a notion of the divine is "necessary for positioning one's finite being in both the context of other finitudes (sexual, social, terrestrial) and in the context of the infinite." The divine offers a figure of perfection and possibility towards which humans can strive in a process of becoming, yet because the Christian God has historically been male, women have been excluded from this project of transcendence: "We have no female trinity. But, as long as woman lacks a divine made in her image she cannot establish her subjectivity or achieve a goal of her own. She lacks an ideal that would be her goal or path in becoming."

Irigaray thus argues that women need an image of the divine that would reflect their own image and encourage their subjectivity. As such, the establishment of a female image of divinity is a necessary condition for relationships of respect between the sexes; "the love of God, for Irigaray, is a love of the self, and this self-love is the prerequisite of love of the other." Only when women are able to claim this subjectivity will they truly be able to relate to men in a non-subordinate relationship of wonder. Cultivating women's subjectivity, or self-love, is the necessary first step towards the full flourishing of all human beings. Thus, this self-love, encouraged by feminine symbols of the divine, is ultimately relational, affecting not only our relationships with ourselves but also with others. Irigaray's emphasis on feminine images of the divine as necessary for women's subjectivity underscores Johnson's own insistence that a fully feminine symbol of God is needed to affirm women's full humanity and promote their flourishing.

Irigaray emphasizes perhaps even more explicitly than Johnson the relational implications of self-love or affirmation encouraged in part by feminine images of the divine. While Johnson does emphasize mutuality and equality, as well as compassion and justice, as results of women's conversation to self-affirmation, Irigaray emphasizes right relations between men and women as the direct result of women's self love. Irigaray first calls for the practice of self-affection, which is a "gathering with ourselves" and "refers to the capability of staying in oneself with a positive feeling." For Irigaray, then, self-affection is encouraged not only by feminine images of the divine but also by this conscious return to ourselves. It enables us to preserve a sense of wholeness and to prepare ourselves for interacting with other people. Without self-affirmation, for Irigaray, there can be no relationships of wonder; if we cannot learn to cultivate and respect a space around ourselves, we will not be able to respect and help cultivate the space around other people. Without self-affirmation, we fall into unjust relationships of possession or control because we will fail to respect the uniqueness and mystery of the other. A return to the self through self-affirmation is "indispensible for the respect of the other." Ultimately, Irigaray emphasizes, perhaps even more than Johnson, the relational implications of women's reclaimed subjectivity.

James Keenan has also emphasized the relational implications of self-care. As we saw in Chapter One, Keenan has offered a reinterpretation of the traditional cardinal virtues of prudence, justice, temperance, and fortitude, offering new virtues based on a more relational anthropology. Keenan's emphasis on self-relating and his virtue of self-care is especially relevant here. For him, this virtue calls us to "care for ourselves, affectively, mentally, physically, and spiritually." Keenan notes that self-esteem is a subcategory of self-care, or one aspect of our overall care for ourselves. I understand self-esteem in the same way as Keenan; self-esteem is one aspect of good self-relating, enabling us to see ourselves as worthy of care. Without self-esteem, our self-care is incomplete, and without self-care we hurt not only ourselves but also our relationships with others.

Johnson, Irigaray, and Keenan all affirm love of self, variously articulated as flourishing, conversion, subjectivity, and self-care, as an essential aspect of our relationship with ourselves and others. Paul Wadell, drawing from Thomas Aquinas, has offered one more permutation: magnanimity. For Thomas, this virtue is a complement to humility. The virtue of magnanimity, as Thomas understands it, complements humility by encouraging a person to aim for great things according to right reason. Whereas humility entails being honest about one's weaknesses, magnanimity entails being honest about one's strengths. It is the virtue of not selling oneself short. The virtue of magnanimity trains us to work for what is best in every dimension of our lives; it does not get sidetracked by lesser, more immediate possibilities, nor is it discouraged in the face of obstacles. Magnanimity, coming from the Latin word for 'greatness,' calls a person to greatness of soul and to use his or her unique gifts confidently and generously. Thomas argues that a magnanimous person has confidence not only in his or herself, but also in others. This virtue thus enables us to see the greatness in ourselves and in others.

Wadell reiterates Thomas' understanding of magnanimity, defining it as "the virtue that trains us to reach for what is best in every dimension of our lives." This virtue challenges us to grow because it calls us to the promising possibility of our lives. Magnanimity calls us not only to recognize our "greatness of soul" but also to act on it. Wadell contrasts magnanimity with pusillanimity, which allows a person to become comfortable with mediocrity by taking the easy way out. Wadell argues that "a pusillanimous life asks nothing of us," whereas a life of magnanimity constantly calls us to have to courage to strive for excellence and to accept "the greatness to which God has called us."

Above we have seen Johnson's emphasis on conversion, self-affirmation, and the empowering symbol of She Who Is; Irigaray's emphasis on the necessity for feminine images of the divine for women's subjectivity and right relations between the sexes; Keenan's understanding of self-esteem as one part of our overall care for ourselves; and Wadell's emphasis on magnanimity as a call to greatness. Based on these contributions, I define the virtue of self-esteem as follows: an aspect of our relationship with ourselves (Keenan) that encourages us to affirm ourselves as full human beings (Wadell, Johnson) and to challenge social and theological attitudes that exclude certain people from full humanity (Irigaray, Johnson). Like wonder, the virtue of self-esteem has two moments—a moment of self-affirmation and a moment of critique that encourages just and mutual relationships.

Applying the Virtue of Self-Esteem

"Start ordaining women or stop dressing like them."
-Women's Ordination Conference bumper sticker

In this section, I first offer some general implications of the virtue of self-esteem, and then show how this virtue can come to bear on the specific issue of the prohibition of women's ordination in the Roman Catholic Church. The virtue of self-esteem has an obvious impact on our relationship with ourselves, but it also impacts our relationships with others, the environment, and God. First, at the level of self-relating, the virtue of self-esteem enables us to have a better self-image and to present that image to others confidently. This virtue encourages us to be confident in our abilities, to be proud of our differences, and to share our gifts with others. Second, at the level of relating to others, the virtue of self-esteem will enable us to relate to others on equal terms, neither feeling inadequate nor feeling the anxious need to dominate. On a broader scale, self-esteem may turn into the pursuit of justice; our own self-confidence may prompt us to work to bring about conditions in which others too can feel self-confident. As Johnson notes, our own "exuberant dignity" calls us "to be creative, self-expressive, and loving together in ways that address human brokenness, violence, and the destruction of the earth."

Third, at the level of our relationship to the earth, the virtue of self-esteem, grounded in the understanding that God not only made *us* good, but *all things* good, will call us to respect the earth as God's beautiful creation. Finally, in our relationship with God, the virtue of self-esteem will allow us to challenge oppressive images of God and to become more aware of God's love for us. Confident in that love, we can let go of our fear of God and see that God takes us and loves us just as we are. With self-esteem comes the recognition of God's own esteem for us.

In addition to these broad applications, the virtue of self-esteem also comes to bear in particular situations, such as the debates over women's ordination in the Roman Catholic Church. In at least the past 40 years, there has been a visible push to ordain Roman Catholic women. Groups such as the Women's Ordination Conference, which was founded in 1975, have worked in various ways to advocate ordination for women. The Roman Catholic Womenpriest movement has been ordaining women as priests and bishops (without official church sanction) since 2002. Despite these and other moves for women's ordination, official church teachings have consistently prohibited such ordinations and have moved to excommunicate members of the Womenpriests.

The most common arguments against women's ordination are that Jesus chose only male disciples, that women cannot represent Christ, and that the church does not have the authority to change an unbroken tradition of ordaining only men. In 1997, the Catholic Theological Society of America (CTSA) published a document questioning the validity of the church's prohibition of women's ordination. This document notes that women were active alongside Jesus during his ministry, as well as in the early church, and contends that it is very doubtful that Jesus intended to exclude women from future church ministry. Further, regarding the long tradition of ordaining only men, the CTSA document notes that most of the traditional arguments against women's ordination are rooted not in scripture but in the belief that women were not suited for ordained ministry because of their inferiority, an argument that is not useful or valid today. The document thus concludes that the teaching against women's ordination "is open to serious theological reinvestigation." The CTSA proceedings and the formation of such groups as the Women's Ordination Conference and the Roman Catholic Womenpriests, along with the support of other Catholic groups such as Call to Action, indicates that there is widespread questioning of the official church teachings against the ordination of women.

Though different groups express their disagreement with the church in different ways— from ordaining women illicitly, to working to change the church from within, to reexamining scriptural and traditional arguments—these movements for women's ordination all demonstrate the virtue of self-esteem in action. Women have begun to recognize that a male-only priesthood is oppressive to women because it does not allow them to follow a call into ministry. They have experienced a moment of self-affirmation, claiming their dignity as full participants in the life of the church in the face of outdated and sexist arguments against their continued prohibition from the priesthood. Beyond this first moment of self-affirmation, they have also initiated the second moment of self-esteem, advocating and working for a change in official church teaching and the full inclusion of women in the sacramental life of the church.

Johnson's symbol of She Who Is plays a role in encouraging women's self-esteem and in advocating for women's ordination. As she argues, the symbol of God has been literalized and patriarchalized, and, by denying women their full status as *imago Dei* and *imago Christi*, has limited women's freedom to fully flourish, especially in the church. The symbol of She Who Is promotes the full equality of women, emphasizing that

women are equally created in the image and likeness of God, equally redeemed by Christ, equally sanctified by the Holy Spirit; women are equally involved in the ongoing tragedy of sin and the mystery of grace, equally called to mission in this world, equally destined for life with God in glory.

Further, as we saw earlier, Johnson takes issue with the argument that women cannot represent Christ because he was a man. She argues that Jesus' maleness belongs to his historical identity—that is, his human identity, and not to his divine one; Jesus' maleness is an accidental characteristic and is not essential to his "redeeming christic identity." The misplacement of Jesus' maleness into his divine redemptive function excludes women from full participation in the church and in the *imago Christi* simply because the physical make up of their bodies is not like Jesus'. Johnson's Jesus-Sophia, on the other hand, offers a more inclusive way of imaging and representing Christ.

In *Beyond God the Father*, Mary Daly notes that women in the church have had the power of naming taken away; women have not been free to use their own power to name God or themselves. The virtue of self-esteem, inspired by She Who Is, encourages women to reclaim this power of naming, to say that we are in the image of God, and to demand fair and equal treatment—in society *and* in the church. Mary Jo Weaver argues that "just in knowing who we are, we will create an upheaval of epic proportions, we will throw the whole system off balance, and we will seriously challenge the future of patriarchal Christianity." Through the virtue of self-esteem suggested by She Who Is, Catholic women can feel empowered to confront church teachings and practices—such as an all-male clergy—that do not allow women their full dignity.

Conclusion

In this chapter, we continued our exploration of some of the ways in which images of God can affect how we understand ourselves and the kinds of characteristics we strive to embody. Emphasizing the importance of women's experiences for theological reflection, Elizabeth Johnson offered us the liberating symbol of She Who Is, while at the same time maintaining that no one image of God should become hegemonic. Johnson's trinitarian theology in turn emphasizes that *all* humans are created in the image of God and that we are called to relationships of mutuality, equality, and compassion. From these anthropological implications, I suggested the virtue of self-esteem, drawn from Johnson's understanding of God, as well as from the work of Irigaray, Keenan, and Wadell. Johnson's symbol of God invites women to consciously practice this virtue of self-esteem—to work on reshaping a more positive self-image; to know that through care and compassion they have the power to bring about a more just society; to cultivate a constant awareness of their likeness to God.

5

The Theology of Catherine Keller

"**I** am folded, and unfolded, and unfolding..."
-Counting Crows, "Colorblind"

In this chapter, we look at the trinitarian work of our final the-ologian, Catherine Keller. Thus far, our theologians have yielded rich material for ethical reflection, and Keller's theology promises to be no different. Born in 1953, Keller is currently a Professor of Constructive Theology at Drew University, and her work has dealt with a range of theological issues, from creation to apocalypse. She draws heav-ily from process theology, the mystical tradition, and feminist theol-ogy in much of her work, and many of her writings promote social and ecological justice. Though she herself is a practicing Methodist, her work reaches across denominational, and even religious, lines. This chapter follows the same pattern as the previous two: first, I ex-amine Keller's theology through the lens of the four sources; I then explore the anthropological implications of her theology, suggest a virtue drawn from the theology, and offer a practical application of the virtue. We begin with Keller's engagement with the four sources in her work on the Trinity.

Keller's Use of the Four Sources

"[W]hat is the actual work of theology—but an incantation at the edge of uncertainty?"

-Catherine Keller, *Face of the Deep*

Unlike Elizabeth Johnson or John Zizioulas, Catherine Keller has not dedicated a large portion of her work directly to the Trinity. Rather, a strand of trinitarian interest runs through her works on other topics, from her early *From a Broken Web* through her most recent writings. This trinitarian strand is most discernible in her *Face of the Deep*, so that is where I will concentrate most of my effort, but I will bring in her other works when they are relevant. In *Face of the Deep*, Keller reconsiders the doctrine of *creatio ex nihilo* (creation out of nothing), suggesting instead *creatio ex profundus*—a creation out of the primal chaos, or *tehom*. Keller offers critiques of the traditional *ex nihilo* doctrine and offers a more fluid interpretation of the creation event; both her critique and her constructive work are prompted in large part by a re-reading of the first two verses of the book of Genesis, as we will see below.

Keller's *creatio ex profundus* has trinitarian implications; in her thought we find not an omnipotent God who creates simply with a snap of the fingers, but a God of interdependence, always already engaged with the world in an "endless process of becoming." Keller names Tehom, the Depth of God and the matrix of possibility, as the first member of a Trinity of folds. This Depth, "ocean of divinity, womb and place-holder of beginnings," is that which folds the world into God. The second member is the Difference of God, that which unfolds continually into the world, ever revealing God in an "incipient incarnation, at the edge of the waters." Thus, Depth as God enfolding all, and Difference as God unfolding into all.

The third member of Keller's Trinity, the Spirit of God, is the relation of relations, "the dynamism of relation itself within a universe in which nothing is what it is in abstraction from the matrix of relations." The Spirit, not transcending difference but connecting through it, suggests not only a divine interdependency but also the interdependence of creator and creation, and of all creatures. Keller's tehomic Trinity—the Depth, the Difference, and the Spirit—is involved in the world in a continual process of creative, relational becoming. This Trinity, whose members "take their divinity with a grain of salt," thus emphasizes interdependence, openness, and creativity, and suggests a theology "in which chaos replaces the nihil and in which flux, carefully mediated by forms of stability, permanence and order, remains primary."

In the following pages, we further explore this tehomic Trinity and the sources from which Keller has drawn to construct it. Keller's writing often reflects her tehomic theology; she draws from many texts and traditions, writes in poetic language, and purposely leaves her arguments open-ended. As Sallie McFague has remarked, "one needs to take a deep breath and to cross one's fingers when attempting to summarize the primary themes or arguments" of Keller's work." As we plunge into the tehomic waters of Keller's theology to find its trinitarian strands, we keep in mind her resistance to orderliness and closure.

SCRIPTURE: THE BOOK OF GENESIS

We can discern an interest in the Trinity running throughout much of Keller's work, finding trinitarian themes in her critiques of traditional doctrines of God, her feminist interpretations of relationality, and her re-thinking of epistemology. Perhaps the most relevant place to begin exploring her understanding of the Trinity, however, is her work on the creation account. *Face of the Deep*, along with the more recent *On the Mystery* and other essays, deals in great detail with the first two verses of the book of Genesis. Keller's use of and engagement with scripture is most obvious in this analysis of Genesis. Thus, in the following sections, I explore her work on Genesis 1:1-2, as well as on the book of Job, as the uses of scripture that come to bear the most on her interpretation of the Trinity. I first briefly discuss Keller's interpretation of the first lines of Genesis. I then show the interplay between scripture and tradition in other interpretations of the creation account before moving to Keller's engagement with the book of Job.

Keller translates the first two verses of Genesis as:

[1]When in the beginning Elohim created heaven and earth, [2]the earth was tohu va bohu, darkness was upon the face of tehom, and the ruach elohim vibrating upon the face of the waters...

She leaves several of the key Hebrew words untranslated. She notes that "tohu va bohu" (typically "formless and void") "remains an indefinable singularity" that could perhaps be translated as "hodge-podge;" "tehom" can be translated as ocean, deep, chaos, or abyss; and "ruach elohim" can be rendered "spirit of God" or "divine spirit." Keller notes that the history of interpretation of these first verses of Genesis, particularly of the second verse, present us with a mystery: "the case of the missing chaos." As we will see in the next section, time and again throughout the Christian tradition, the chaos (*tehom*) present in the second verse of Genesis has been ignored, repressed, or ridiculed. Keller, on the other hand, offers an interpretation of this verse that acknowledges and values that chaos as a source of creativity. She further notes the feminine origins of *tehom*, showing how the rejection of the chaos goes hand-in-hand with the subordination of women. She argues that the Hebrew "*tehom*" is feminine, and further, that the writer of the first verses of Genesis uses it without an article, as one would a proper name.

Drawing from other scholars, Keller argues that the feminine figure of *tehom* in Genesis is related to the feminine figure of Tiamat in the Babylonian creation story, *Enuma Elish*. In the *Enuma Elish*, Tiamat is slaughtered by the great male hero, Marduk, who imposes order on the universe. In Genesis, on the other hand, *tehom* remains mysteriously present and unconquered by any "hero." As we will see, however, in subsequent interpretations of these first verses of Genesis, *tehom* suffers the same fate as Tiamat—she is slaughtered by those wishing "to master the chaos, perchance to destroy it, to flush it from the universe." Keller argues that interpretations of Genesis 1:1-2 that erase the chaos are thus guilty of *tehomophobia*: "Fear of whatever shadows our light, whatever transgresses boundaries, leaks across categories, sneaks out of closets, whatever she-sea might suddenly flood our fragile confidence. Fear of the 'female thing.' Of all things too deep and too fluid: we may call this fear *tehomophobia.*" Both scripture and tradition play an important role in the interpretation, both tehomophobic and tehomophilic, of the first verses of Genesis; in the next section I show how Keller engages each of these sources in her work specifically on Genesis. Later, I continue to examine Keller's other uses of scripture and her engagement with other aspects of tradition.

SCRIPTURE AND TRADITION: *CREATIO EX NIHILO*

As we have seen, in *Face of the Deep* Keller reinterprets the first two verses of the book of Genesis to offer an interpretation of creation as *ex profundus*—out of the depths—rather than *ex nihilo*—out of nothing. In this work, Keller engages the theologies of Irenaeus, Athanasius, Augustine, and Karl Barth, showing how these thinkers contributed to the doctrine of *creatio ex nihilo* and how they deal with (or ignore) the "watery depths" of the second verse of Genesis.

According to Keller, the position of *creatio ex nihilo* began its ascent to orthodox doctrine in the late second century with Irenaeus, the Bishop of Lyons. Irenaeus establishes his theology of creation through a complicated conversation with gnosticism. Keller points to a gnostic creation myth involving a number of emanations, or Aeons, from God, who then take on their own personalities and roles in the creation of the world. The world itself is created out of the miscarried body of Achamoth, the daughter of Wisdom. The gnostic creation myth, then, involves both a plurality of divine figures and the creation of the world out of a female figure. Irenaeus, Keller suggests, took issue with both of these aspects of the gnostic theology; such a theology divides "the One rational and indivisible Creator into a monstrous hybrid, materializing in multiple, sensual, and emotional figurations." Irenaeus opts for a tidier, less ambiguous creation event, positing creation out of nothing by the Father, who is omnipotent and not in need of the mediating Aeons. This account of the creation is clear-cut, in contrast to the messiness and ambiguity (and feminine undertones) of the gnostic account, pointing to the Father's self-sufficiency and power, thus laying the foundations for the doctrine of *creatio ex nihilo.*

Later, in the mid-fourth century, Keller argues, Athanasius further shored up the orthodox standing of the *creatio ex nihilo.* Athanasius takes issue with a platonic understanding of creation that posits a pre-existent material that God then shapes into the world. According to Keller, he argues that this creation story makes God weak, since "he" is dependent on material "he" did not create. For Athanasius, a God who fashions the universe out of pre-existent material is more like a craftsperson than a powerful creator. Keller notes that Athanasius makes no reference to the second verse of Genesis and that he "deliberately conceals chaos." In addition to Athanasius' firm rejection of a creation out of pre-existent matter, there is also a strong anti-heretical emphasis in his writings, both of which help to shore up the idea of creation *ex nihilo* by establishing it as doctrine and excluding other interpretations of the creation event. In both Irenaeus and Athanasius, Keller argues, we see a suppression of the chaos of creation found in Genesis. As Keller describes the work of these church fathers:

In their triumphant logos we have read a logic whereby the creation doctrine guards God's unity against gnostic complexity; unconditional omnipotence against constraining conditions; masculine symbolic privilege against all maternalized chaos; a Creator who 'begets' against any who procreate; the monosexual celibate elite against same-sex temptation; the closure of canon against uncontrolled textual multiplication; the ascendency of imperial narrative of a single Logos against the confusion of competing narratives.

The logic of an omnipotent, masculine, orderly God , developed early in the church's history, continues to dominate the Christian tradition.

Keller also traces the theme of depth through Augustine's *Confessions,* reading his work as neither tehomophobic nor tehomophilic. For example, Augustine references the deep in his baptismal imagery; in his words, "this is the spirit which from the beginning 'moved upon the face of the waters.' For neither can the Spirit act without the water, nor the water without the Spirit." He further imagines God as a great ocean, with creation as a sponge soaking up and suffused with the water that is God. Keller suggests that Augustine's autobiographical *Confessions,* in addition to using oceanic imagery, also focus on the depths within the self. In the *Confessions,* Keller argues, "tehom gets interiorized" as Augustine struggles with the darkness and shame he feels within himself. Yet these interior depths are not always bad; sometimes they are experienced as a flood of sin, yet other times as an ocean of divinity. Keller thus argues that Augustine expresses a "tehomic ambivalence," sublimating rather than suppressing the chaos.

Finally, Keller turns to the *ex nihilo* in the work of Karl Barth, an early twentieth-century Reformed theologian. *Tehom* does not fare well in Barth: "If the early fathers repress the dark waters, if Augustine more indulgently sublimates them, Barth's opus performs their demonization...The Barthian deep is not nothing, but worse than nothing." Barth interprets the deep as the nothingness to which God said 'no' in the act of creation. Unlike Irenaeus or Athanasius, who tend to overlook the second verse of Genesis, Barth attends carefully to the scriptural text. Aware of the chaos of verse 2, he argues that the doctrine of *ex nihilo* does not fit the biblical narrative, so he rejects it. He also rejects, as does Athanasius, creation out of pre-existent material that is independent of God. Thus Keller notes that she and Barth have something in common—they both seek a third way to interpret the creation story. They do not, however, agree on what this third way is.

According to Keller, Barth reads the second verse of Genesis as "a parody of pagan mother-goddess imagery." Barth reads the chaotic waters as an offense to heaven, that which is excluded from existence, and the Spirit brooding above those waters as an impotent hoax; "so the impotent bird hovers over sterile waters" in a parody of pagan creation myths. As Keller notes, Barth's God creates not *out of nothing* but *against the nothingness* of those vaguely feminine, sterile waters. As we will see in later sections, Keller's own interpretation of these verses in Genesis, unlike Barth's, plunges into those very waters as the source of creativity and possibility.

Though Keller critiques the development of the *ex nihilo* doctrine, she does note the importance of attending to traditional thought:

Why return to these old paternal cosmo-polemics? I suggested that theology has no choice but to return recurrently and critically to its originative discourses—unless it wants to create theology *ex nihilo*. If we do not content ourselves with an ahistorical origin, beginnings matter.

Keller's exploration of the chaos, or deep, in the second verse of Genesis comes to bear on her understanding of the Trinity. As we will see, her Trinity enfolds and unfolds into the world, reflecting not a God of independence and omnipotence, but rather one who lures creation into interdependent and cooperative being.

SCRIPTURE: THE BOOK OF JOB

In addition to a careful analysis of Genesis 1:1-2, Keller also looks closely at the book of Job for further insights into the lost chaos. The book of Job recounts the story of a pious man, Job, who endures both the death of his sons and his own physical suffering. Job's friends visit him, at first sitting with him in his suffering, and, after seven days, offering explanations for Job's suffering. The general consensus among these friends is that Job must have sinned in order to have received such punishment from God. Job, however, convinced of his innocence, desires a better explanation; why would God punish an innocent man? Finally, Job is visited by God in the form of a whirl-wind, who then offers a lengthy speech in response to Job's questioning. Keller notes that this speech can be read tehomophobically, as a display of force to silence Job's questions ("the whirlwind is a windbag"), but her own interpretation is more tehomophilic. Reading God's speech to Job as an "exegetical iteration of the creation narrative," Keller argues that the divine mystery present in the whirlwind delights in creation but neither takes responsibility for Job's suffering nor claims omnipotence. Rather, the God in the whirlwind "claims responsibility for the broad sweep of the universe...but not for any specific events in the lives of people." The tehomic God of Job, as Keller reads it, does not bring about the suffering of humans and offers no easy answers; "in a universe of open-ended indeterminacy, in which our most wounded questions rarely yield direct answers, faith will approximate as courage."

In the last sections, we have seen how Keller has engaged and critiqued the traditional interpretations of Genesis 1:1-2, highlighting the importance of the often overlooked *tehom*, as well as her reading of the book of Job, which continues her emphasis on mystery and open-endedness. In Keller's tehomic reading of scripture, the Bible's "metaphors, signs, and parables are not stripped of their poetry and indirection." We have also seen Keller's examination of how four major thinkers in the Christian tradition—Irenaeus, Athanasius, Augustine, and Barth—contributed to the development of the doctrine of *creatio ex nihilo*. In the next section, we examine Keller's broader use of the Christian tradition and the aspects of it from which she draws to further emphasize chaos and interdependency.

TRADITION

In general, Keller draws mainly from process theology and the apophatic tradition in her constructive work on the Trinity. Process thought finds its roots in Alfred North Whitehead, a twentieth-century mathematician-turned-philosopher. He sought to connect the insights of Einstein's theory of relativity and new insights from quantum physics with everyday life. The result was an "elaborate rethinking of the universe as one immense, living, and open-ended network of spontaneous interactions." Process theology grew out of Whitehead's philosophical work and is associated with such thinkers as Charles Hartshorne, John Cobb, and Marjorie Suchocki. Keller herself studied with John Cobb and the Center for Process Studies at Claremont Graduate University and has continued to engage process theology throughout her academic career.

Keller highlights radical relationality—among humans, between humans and the world, between humans and God, and within God—as one central tenet of process theology. Keller has engaged this issue of relationality in nearly all of her work. In her early work, *From a Broken Web*, for example, Keller notes the dangerous ways in which relationality has been gendered; men have been taught to be too individualistic, while women have been taught to lose themselves in relationships. She points to the myth of the archetypal hero, whose "philosophical descendant is the separate, self-enclosed subject, remaining self-identical throughout its exploits of time." Alongside this separative self, which tends to define men, we have the soluble self, which tends to define women. This soluble self cannot define herself; she must, rather, wait for her self-definition to be given to her by men. Keller argues that a new kind of relationality is needed to overcome the separative-soluble relationship among selves. Keller emphasizes interdependence among persons and argues that the separative self is an illusion. In contrast, the soluble self dissolves too much into relation and does not hold on to any individual self-definition. A mean between too much relationality and too little, one that emphasizes both individuality and interdependence, is needed to correct sexist and oppressive relationships between men and women.

Keller's work on the creation account in *Face of the Deep* and *On the Mystery* also deals with the radical relationality of process theology. She suggests that God is "a living process of interaction...The mystery may be addressed with metaphors of eros, of flow, of illimitable inter-activity, or open ends and unknowable origins, of immeasurable ma-terialization;" Keller's process God remains bound up with the world. In short, she argues, process theology posits that "the alternative to impotence lies in the risky interactivity of relationship." This is true of human-God, human-human, human-world, and intradivine rela-tionships; we are all—God, humans, the universe—bound up with each other.

While Keller draws from some of the main themes of process the-ology, like radical relationality, she notes that she employs it "in a mul-tivalent and fluid sense, more tinged with mysticism, more freighted with scriptural narrative." We have already seen how Keller engages scripture; below we see how, in addition to process theology, she draws from the apophatic theology of the mystical tradition. Like Elizabeth Johnson, Keller notes that "the challenge of naming the un-namable" opens space for many metaphors, and she turns to negative theology for further insights into the mysteriousness of God. Draw-ing from Dorothee Söelle, Meister Eckhart, and Nicholas of Cusa, Keller offers a way of unknowing—of purposely letting go of what we think we know. Such an unknowing both enables a new perspec-tive on the traditional interpretation of the Genesis creation account and encourages more comfort with mystery—the mystery of God, of the universe, and of being human. Thus for Keller, "mysticism means, as the word itself hints, not primarily special experiences or esoteric gifts, but a persistent attunement to mystery."

Keller draws most heavily from Nicholas of Cusa's negative theol-ogy, or what he termed "sacred ignorance." Cusa insisted on the way of unknowing—of letting go of all of our names for and attributes of God—as the way to truly reverence the infinite mystery of God. From Cusa, Keller draws an "apophatic epistemology of unknowing," which she employs throughout much of her work, avoiding too orderly an approach and resisting drawing definite conclusions.

More specific to the trinitarian strands in her work, Keller draws from Cusa's theology of folds. Cusa offers an understanding of "the dynamic contracting, or *complicatio* ("enfolding") and *explicatio* ("unfolding") of God and the universe into each other, and that of the radical interrelatedness of creatures;" Cusa's God enfolds and unfolds into the world. Keller, drawing from Gilles Deleuze, a 20th century French philosopher, adds *implicatio* to Cusa's *compilcatio* and *explicatio* to suggest a Trinity of folds. Not trinitarian "persons" in the traditional sense, Keller's Trinity is one rather of relational capacities. The *complicatio*, which in Cusa's thought is the folding together of God and the world, is the first of these capacities and corresponds to Tehom—the depth of God. The folding together then gives rise to an unfolding—Cusa's *explicatio*—of the world out of God in "pulsations of divergence." This *explicatio* corresponds to Elohim as the *difference* of God unfolding into creation; *complicatio* as all enfolded into God and *explicatio* as God unfolding into all. To these two, Keller adds a third, *implicatio,* or relationality itself, relating "the divine interdependency to the interdependencies of the world." This *implicatio* corresponds to Sophia as the *Spirit* of God; "*Ruach* on the face of the waters: it has provided the pulsing, folding force of a tehomic theology all along."

At the risk of a too organized account of Keller's Trinity, below I offer a chart of the various terms she uses to describe the trinitarian capacities:

Complicatio	*Explicatio*	*Implicatio*

Depth of God	Difference of God	Spirit of God
Enfolds	Unfolds	Differentiates and connects
Tehom	Elohim	Sophia

Keller combines her use of the process and mystical traditions to offer what she variously calls a tehomic theology, poststructuralist process theology, or apophatic panentheism. As we saw in the last chapter, panentheism envisions a God intimately involved with, yet not identical to, the world: "The *"en"*[in 'panentheism] designates an active indeterminacy, a commingling of unpredictable, and yet recapitulatory, self-organizing relations. The *"en"* asserts the difference of divine and cosmic, but at the same time makes it impossible to draw the line." Nothing—not humans, not the cosmos, not God—is immune from interdependency or indeterminacy; "the tehomic deity remains enmeshed in the vulnerabilities and potentialities of an indeterminate creativity." Keller's is a theology of enfolding and unfolding, of a God intimately involved with the world, of allowing oneself to be pulled into the deep, of surrendering to the mystery of God; "the world is not your oyster. It is your ocean."

In addition to drawing from the process and apophatic traditions to offer a process Trinity, Keller also offers a creative interpretation of the traditional trinitarian doctrine. In an essay of hers, "Burning Tongues: A Feminist Trinitarian Epistemology," for example, she explores how our understanding of each traditional person of the Trinity (Father, Son, Holy Spirit) can affect our ways of knowing. The first person, traditionally designated 'Father,' she argues, was not intended to suggest a literally male God; rather, the term suggests the fact that God is not an object but a person, that is, a relational being. Keller argues that the personhood implied by the 'Father' has epistemological implications for us—because God is personal, we come to know things through our own experiences as persons.

For Keller, the second person of the Trinity, traditionally the 'Son,' highlights the relational nature of our knowing. She argues that what we admire about Christ is not his individual heroism but the quality of the relationships he generated around him; Jesus' relationships were characterized by compassion, forgiveness, and respect. Christ's example reminds us that we are "members of one another," and that our ways of knowing are bound up with our relationships.

Finally, the third person, the 'Spirit,' signifies the relation of relations, "the dynamism of relation itself." For Keller, the Spirit is always present in our relationships; thus the Spirit's qualities are immediacy and presence. This suggests that our knowing also is in the present; we know what our bodies and our relationships can tell us in the here and now.

In this section, we have seen how Keller engages process theology and the apophatic tradition in constructing her tehomic theology, in which the trinitarian capacities enfold and unfold among each other and the world. We also saw how Keller's epistemological interpretation of the traditional trinitarian figures highlights the personal, relational, and present nature of our knowing.

SECULAR DISCIPLINES

Keller makes extensive use of the secular disciplines in her work, drawing from such sources as chaos theory, quantum physics, literary criticism, poststructuralism, and feminist theory. In the section below, I briefly touch on Keller's use of these secular disciplines as they come to bear on her understanding of the Trinity.

First, Keller engages some of the discoveries and theories of modern science, such as chaos theory and quantum physics. She notes that the term 'chaos,' in chaos theory, designates not total disorder but rather "a process unfolding unpredictably and yet with organization." Chaos math and science, according to Keller, depict complex forms of flow, too complex to be captured in a linear formula but not formless or completely disorderly. The chaos of chaos theory thus parallels that of Genesis 1:2; neither ordered nor disordered, the "monstrously untidy creativity" of *tehom* unfolds as a matrix of possibility, life-giving yet unpredictable.

Keller also draws from the strange world of quantum physics, which has contributed, among other things, the uncertainty principle and the possible existence of mysterious dark matter. The uncertainty principle, coined by Werner Heisenberg in 1927, claims that we cannot accurately determine both the speed and the location of a subatomic particle (e.g., an electron). That is, we can know where it is, but not how fast it is moving, or we can know how fast it is moving, but not where it is. This principle can be unsettling, especially for scientists who are used to being able to provide precise, definite answers. The evidence of dark matter likewise introduces a mysterious and indefinable element into the universe, thwarting once again our desire for clear-cut, tidy answers and reminding us of the limits of our knowledge. No one knows what dark matter is—no one has seen it, touched it, or observed it—but scientists think that perhaps as much of three-quarters of the universe is "composed of this darkness over the face of the deep of space." This dark matter, the uncertainty principle, and chaos theory, among other scientific contributions, help inform Keller's theology, which echoes the complexity, uncertainty, and mystery of modern science. As she herself puts it, "insistently pluralist, tuned to the echo of the earth and the scales of the heavens, curious rather than defensive towards the sciences, this becoming-theology makes itself at home within complexity."

In addition to drawing from the sciences, Keller also draws from literature, offering an analysis of *Moby Dick* in *Face of the Deep*. *Moby Dick,* written by the American Herman Melville in 1851, is narrated by Ishmael, a sailor who takes a voyage on the whaling ship *Pequod* and witnesses the captain Ahab's obsessive quest to kill the white sperm whale, Moby Dick, who had taken Ahab's leg in a previous encounter. Keller draws on themes of mystery and the desire for control from *Moby Dick,* adding more depth to her own tehomic theology. The narrator Ishmael, for example, initiates a lengthy process of trying to completely describe the whale, only to find that the whale remains elusive and indescribable:

Any way you look at it, you must needs conclude that the great Leviathan is that one creature in the world which must remain unpainted to the last. True, one portrait may hit the mark much nearer than another, but none can hit it with any very considerable degree of exactness. So there is no earthly way of finding out precisely what the whale really looks like.

Keller also focuses on Ishmael's description of the *whiteness* of the whale and Melville's thoughts on race, as we will see in a later section.

Keller also notes Captain Ahab's monomaniacal quest for revenge on Moby Dick. Ahab's obsession is all-consuming and tragic; he must have his revenge and exert his control over the whale, but his quest leads only to his own death. Ahab's obsession is reflected in his cry: "towards thee I roll, thou all-destroying but unconquering whale; to the last I grapple with thee; from hell's heart I stab at thee; for hate's sake I spit my last breath at thee." Ahab, afraid of what lurks beneath the surface and determined to control and subdue it, is an example of Keller's tehomophobia in action. She notes that Ahab's tragic quest in *Moby Dick* has a lesson: "Make the unfathomable your fear—and your suicide can become omnicide. Make the untamed universe your enemy—it will blankly oblige."

Finally, in addition to the sciences and literature, Keller draws from the secular disciplines of continental philosophy and poststructuralist and feminist theory. Drawing from and influenced by such thinkers as Gilles Deleuze, Jacques Derrida, Luce Irigaray, Judith Butler, Emmanuel Levinas, and Julia Kristeva, Keller demonstrates a firm grasp of the western philosophical tradition, though she has been criticized for drawing somewhat haphazardly from that tradition. Corey Walker, for example, suggests that "the very *multiplicity* that grounds and animates [*Face of the Deep*] necessarily invokes the specter of insufficient attention to the depth of detail, particularly with regards to some aspects of her theoretical formulations and the implications for her theological project." Indeed, allusions to these and other thinkers appear on nearly every page of Keller's works, which has prompted Sallie McFague to suggest reading Keller's *Face of the Deep* "as you would good (but somewhat difficult) poetry—ready to catch the insights you can (and let the rest go)." Despite the difficulty of Keller's frequent, sometimes obscure, sometimes seemingly haphazard references to postmodern and feminist theory, her use of these secular disciplines does contribute to her overall project. Whether it is a deconstructive technique drawn from Derrida, an emphasis on fluidity drawn from Irigaray, or an intentional open-endedness about what it means to be human drawn from Butler, these and other thinkers add depth and new perspectives to Keller's already deep and insightful work.

Neither, as Walker might suggest, does Keller appropriate these sources uncritically. Indeed, though Keller makes use of postmodern and feminist theory in her work, she has also paused "to consider a feminist theological tendency to emulate too uncritically certain assumptions" of such theories. For example, she has noted a tendency to be skeptical of some feminist theories of relationality because they are perceived to run the risk of essentializing women. In other words, Keller argues, because women have historically been associated, in ways that were harmful to them, with being the more relational sex (as she shows in *From a Broken Web*), any new feminist theory of re-lationality is automatically considered suspect. Relational theories are automatically and uncritically flagged as essentializing and as rein-scribing traditional harmful understandings of women as the "rela-tional sex." Keller notes such tendencies in secular feminist theorists, such as Julia Kristeva, and argues that some Christian feminists, such as Elizabeth Schüssler Fiorenza, have followed suit. She notes that both secular and Christian feminists have eschewed theories of re-lationality or interdependency in favor of a "postmodern individual-ism," which then tends to reinforce the harmful distinction between male/control/individualism and female/weakness/relationality.

Keller argues that in order to "outgrow the androcentric discourse of separation and independence, we need to understand that con-nectivity cannot be equated with femininity or dependency. Rela-tionalist insight needs maturation through constructive criticism, not abandonment." In short, Keller argues that, in their well-intentioned avoidance of essentializing, some secular feminist theorists and the Christian feminists who appropriate them too uncritically have failed to see how critical theories of relationality can contribute positively to feminist theory. While Keller makes extensive use of postmodern secular feminist theory in her work, then, she also notes its shortcom-ings.

In this section, we saw how Keller's engagement with the secular disciplines of modern science, literary criticism, and poststructuralist and feminist theory enrich her own tehomic theology. Her use of these disciplines confirms and further emphasizes the themes of chaos, depth, relationality, and *tehomophobia* in her work. We have also seen how some thinkers have critiqued the sometimes obscure references and sheer number of thinkers and theories Keller engages. As Laurel Schneider wrote of *Face of the Deep*, Keller's work is "flawed by the things that make it brilliant. I wished at times for both less and more: less flash and more pause; less gesture towards justice and more of its messy realization; less crowding of voices and texts and more calm boldness in her own voice." Despite the difficulty of reading some of her work, Keller adeptly engages secular disciplines of knowledge and employs them creatively to supplement her tehomic theology.

EXPERIENCE

It is difficult to determine just how Keller engages experience in constructing her theology. Unlike Elizabeth Johnson, for example, she does not explicitly draw from experience as a source for her theology. That is not to say, however, that experience does not play a role in her work. Indeed, her process panentheism subtly draws from and confirms the experiences of many Christian women (and men). For example, her tehomic theology, Keller would argue, is better equipped than traditional theology to address both the experience of suffering and the experience of the messiness of our own lives. As we saw in her discussion of the book of Job, traditional understandings of God's omnipotence fall short when we experience suffering; if God can do anything, why does God allow suffering, or worse, cause people to suffer? Keller notes that, in these moments of intense suffering, "when faith is most urgently needed, the logic of omnipotence lays upon naked suffering the added burden of godforsakenness." Keller's tehomic theology, on the other hand, offers no facile answers to the problem of suffering; her God does not cause suffering or simply allow it to happen but is, rather, compassionately present with us in our suffering. Keller's account, then, offers perhaps a more realistic response to the experience of suffering.

Keller's tehomic theology also reflects more realistically and confirms the experience of the messiness or chaos in our own lives. Within the logic of many traditional accounts, God is an all-powerful, organizing force who has total control over "his" environment; this image of an "in-control" God then encourages people to seek control over their own lives. We are taught to be orderly, to "have it together," to be self-sufficient and not ask for help. While some degree of order and self-sufficiency in our lives is necessary, such an ethos teaches us to fear being out of control and to keep the untidiness of our lives hidden from others. We are not to let on that our lives may be spinning out of control. Keller's tehomic theology, on the other hand, encourages us to embrace the inevitable chaos that surfaces in our lives and to engage it rather than fear it. Keller's God is neither perfectly orderly nor disorderly but rather complexly ordered or creatively chaotic; the deep is not total chaos but a matrix of possibility. Keller's theology thus enables us to deal more openly and creatively with our experiences of feeling out of control.

Further, Keller does not affirm this chaos (either the chaos of creation or the chaos within ourselves) as unambiguously good; too much chaos can destroy us. She thus reads *tehom*

...as the active potentiality *for both good and evil*. So the capacity to resist any order, even a divine order, belongs to its indeterminacy. It gives rise to the destructive chaos in the universe as surely as—with divine wisdom—it gives birth to the beauties of complex order. Even a tehomophilic reading of verse 2 does not declare the chaos itself 'good.'

Keller's theology thus notes a disconnect between certain human experiences and traditional theology. Whereas some more traditional theologies insist on God's power and control, Keller's theology responds to our experiences of suffering and chaos by offering a vision of a God of compassionate presence who bears with and engages the chaos, calling us to do the same.

FEMINIST PERSPECTIVES ON KELLER'S THEOLOGY

"Seymour once said to me—in a crosstown bus of all places—that all legitimate religious study *must* lead to unlearning the differences, the illusory differences, between boys and girls, animals and stones, day and night, heat and cold."

-J.D. Salinger, *Franny and Zooey*

There are few feminist critiques of Keller's thought that relate to her understanding of the Trinity. She herself, though, has written an essay about the ways in which feminist theology has unfolded and ought to be unfolding. In this essay, written in 2008, Keller reflects on the state of feminist theology, addressing both the influence of secular theory and the ways in which race, class, and sexuality have all complicated feminists' work on gender. After briefly overviewing her arguments in this essay, I then apply its insights to her work on the Trinity, essentially letting Keller critique herself.

In her 2008 essay, Keller first notes that feminist theology "talks back" not only to Christian theologians, many of whom question how one can be a feminist and a Christian, but also to secular feminists, many of whom question why one would want to be a Christian at all. She then notes four "folds" of feminist theology—the gender fold, the color-fold, and queer fold, and the manifold—each of which involves "a certain undoing of gender." With these four folds, which do not necessarily correspond to historical movements but rather keep folding and unfolding, Keller highlights the multiplicity of intersecting contexts and sites of difference that complicate ("fold together") our understandings of gender. First, the gender fold initially unfolds as "an affirmation of woman" but oftentimes ends up affirming only middle-class white American women. Thus the color-fold folds into gender to bring to the surface the voices of women of color. The folding together of gender and race continues not only "to unsay the sexist prejudices but also the feminist presumptions" of well-to-do white women. The folds do not stop with gender and color; sexuality too comes into the fold, undoing the heteronormativity of earlier feminist theory. This queer fold affirms lesbian, gay, bisexual, and transgendered persons as "another set of humans whose very being had been negated by the norms of the normal" even as it "wrinkles them with multiplicities and ambiguities," undoing the binaries of gay/straight and man/woman.

From these gender, color, and queer folds unfurls the manifold, "the particular multiplicity which our unfolding at a particular moment requires," which folds in the untidiness of our relationality and the ways in which we have been shaped, even unknowingly, by all of our relationships. In this manifold, we are all folded in together with the earth, and, recognizing that we "fold in and out of each other moment by moment," we seek to undo the violence (gendered, colored, sexual) that we have experienced or perpetrated. And even after these four folds, the folds keep unfolding; the folded oppressions continue to unfold and be negated as we realize more and more our interconnectedness and fully affirm ourselves and one another, regardless of the complexities and the differences in our genders, colors, sexualities, nationalities, abilities, etc; "the tender word of the gospels did not come to ask: with what kind of body are you making love? But only: *are you loving?*"

How does Keller's work on the Trinity deal with these four folds—gender, color, queer, and manifold? Keller argues that the gender fold is primarily an affirmation of women. We saw this kind of affirmation perhaps most clearly in the work of Elizabeth Johnson, whose image of She Who Is clearly affirms women as being in the image of God. Keller's affirmation of women is more subtle; her tehomic Trinity—the Deep, the Difference, and the Spirit—does not immediately call to mind women as *imago Dei* in the way that Johnson's theology does. Nonetheless, Keller's emphasis on recovering the deep—that feminine *tehom*, repressed, scorned, and forgotten throughout Christian history and calling to mind the murdered Tiamat—is both an affirmation of women and a rejection of the logic of control, power, and order.

Keller takes the color fold seriously, reflecting, for example, on the *whiteness* of the whale in *Moby Dick*. Keller reads the narrator Ishmael's description of the whiteness of the whale as a "projection of the horrors of whiteness;" in his description he notes not only that white can be identified with honor but also that whiteness can cause panic or horror, such as in the case of an albino. Keller further notes Ishmael's observation that whiteness is not so much a color but the absence of color. This observation, coupled with what scholars have uncovered about Melville's own abolitionist views, leads Keller to argue that

to make whiteness visible is to learn to read its absent presence: concretely, its racial construction that—until we *see* it—colors myself as white while denying that I have color in the same stroke—truly a colorless all-color. The western dominion over all that can be colored Other has classified the variegated, vivid, dark others—human and nonhuman—of a non-classifiable chaos.

Thus, all people of color are classified as "not white," a chaotic mix of color. Moby Dick, then, the white whale, comes to represent whiteness itself, which "becomes sinister because it goes unrecognized, unacknowledged in its sociosymbolic construction."

In addition to the gender and color folds, Keller also folds in the queer fold. For Keller, homophobia is a part of the ambiguous, feminine, interdependent stuff that *tehomophobia* rejects in favor of a doctrine of power and control; "*tehomophobia* never exceeds its constitutive *homophobia* by much." Like her affirmation of women, though, Keller's affirmation of queer (non-heterosexual) people is subtle. She does not, for example, offer us the "queer God" that Marcella Althaus-Reid does (as we saw in the second chapter). Her *tehomophilic* Trinity does, nonetheless, affirm the experiences of queer people by questioning the narratives of white, male, heterosexual dominance.

Finally, we come to the manifold—all the folds that keep unfolding. Keller's emphasis on radical relationality emphasizes the interdependencies that we begin to recognize in the manifold. Her Trinity is one of folding and unfolding differences, and the manifold encourages a similar unfolding of differences. While she specifically addresses some of these differences, such as gender and race, others are only mentioned in passing. How, for example, can her tehomic Trinity help encourage us to unfold and address prejudices against disabled persons? In all, Keller's theology opens space for the unfolding of many kinds of differences, though she herself does not address them all in depth.

LOOKING FORWARD

In the above sections we have seen how Keller engages the four sources of scripture, tradition, secular disciplines, and experience in constructing her theology. Offering an interpretation of Genesis 1:1-2 that acknowledges and values *tehom*, Keller draws from the process and apophatic traditions, as well as from science, literature, and feminist theory to offer us a Trinity of folds, intimately involved with the world, interdependent, and engaging rather than fearing the chaos. In the next section, we explore the implications Keller's tehomic Trinity has for how we understand ourselves.

Anthropological Implications of Keller's Theology

"I say unto you: one must still have chaos in oneself to be able to give birth to a dancing star. I say unto you: you still have chaos in yourselves."

-Friedrich Nietzsche, *Thus Spake Zarathustra*

"The Deep, the Difference, and the Spirit. The *godness* of our depths, our differences, our spirits." The trinitarian threads running through Keller's work contribute to theological anthropology in two major, interrelated ways: her emphasis on relationality and the openness of her tehomic theology. I explore each of these in turn.

First, Keller's critique of more traditional accounts of the Trinity emphasizes the sometimes forgotten relationality at the heart of the doctrine. Though she critiques, with most feminist theologians, the overwhelmingly masculine attributes of traditional understandings of the Trinity, she does also note that, "for all its arcane chauvinisms," the doctrine of the Trinity perhaps offers the best "possibility of co-constitutive relations between subjects." The traditional interpretations, at their best, reveal "an interdependence at the heart of reality," that in turn emphasizes the more particular interdependencies between humans and God, among humans themselves, and between humans and the world. This relational existence, reflecting the relationality within God, calls us to examine our relationships and to discern which ones may be harmful. Radical relationality is a risky business, as many of our thinkers have noted; our relationships can be enriching, affirming, and life-giving, or they can be destructive, oppressive, and, literally, lethal. Acknowledging our interdependency, then, is not enough, and we are called to distinguish "between suffering that can only be comforted and suffering whose causes can be eradicated." That is, suffering caused by unjust or oppressive relationships can and ought to be eradicated.

Keller's emphasis on the ultimately relational nature of the traditional understanding of the Trinity underscores the need to move beyond the separative and the soluble self. The soluble self dissolves into its relationships, opening itself to abuse, while the separative self operates under the illusion of its self-sufficiency. The traditional trinitarian persons offer a vision of a third kind of self, one that can remain somewhat self-contained yet fully aware of its interdependencies. Keller offers an understanding of a selfhood with fluid boundaries, neither self-sufficient nor dissolved into relationship; "it may be handy, healthy, even life-saving to draw boundaries—until, that is, we deny how relative, how fluid, how permeable the borders remain."

The second major theme in Keller's trinitarian strands that has implications for moral anthropology is her emphasis on recovering the lost chaos of creation. Sallie McFague asks, "if we saw God not as the absolute, distant Creator and Master of the universe, but as the One from whose depths all things emerge and with whose help creatures reach fulfillment, might our theologies (as well as our pastoral work and politics) find a new paradigm?" Keller's tehomic theology offers us one possible answer to this question. As we saw in the section of Keller's use of experience as a source, her tehomic Trinity creatively

embraces the chaos; an open-ended, untidy, panentheistic God likewise encourages us to let go of our fear of disorder and our illusions of
control. A tehomic anthropology, just as a tehomic theology, requires
us to bear with the chaos:

We may feel shame before the chaos in our lives, families, sexualities, movements, ethnicities, drafts, projects. Or we may read this
difficult milieu for its freshly emerging order. If we do not try to control what seems out of control, if rather we brood on the fluid face,
the *eschaton* between what is too chaotic and what is too limiting, we
will discern the specific possibility of the transition.

Both of these anthropological implications of Keller's theology—an emphasis on relationality and an embrace of the chaos—involve risk. The radical relationality and chaotic depth of Keller's
Trinity highlight the risks and realities of being in relationship and
of letting go of control (or the illusion of control). Embracing our interdependencies and messiness opens us not only to good but also to
more suffering. It will take "great discernment to know the difference."

All three of our theologians—John Zizioulas, Elizabeth Johnson,
and Catherine Keller—have emphasized relationality as both a central
divine and human characteristic. Zizioulas offers a relational ontology
of triune and human personhood; Johnson offers a God of mutual and
equal relationships that affirms women's experience; Keller offers a
God of interdependence who calls us to feel at home in the chaos of
our own lives and relationships. Keller's tehomic Trinity is one who
creates in the midst of chaos, who both unfolds into the world and enfolds the world back into itself; if we are in the image of this God, we
will do well to recognize our own interdependence—both with each
other and with the created world—and we will accept the fact that our
lives are messy and chaotic. Keller's Trinity sits with ambiguity and
creates out of it; so should we. In fact, it is only within the chaos—the
Deep—that creation is possible at all; God creates "not 'out of nothing'
but 'in the midst of everything.'" Keller's tehomic Trinity confronts us

with the 'deep' in our own lives, calling us to engage it and to create out of it, all the while reminding us that "we are always in over our heads."

Keller's Theology and the Virtue of Open-Endedness

"And I shall not grow weary of becoming."
-Antoine de St Exupéry, *The Wisdom of the Sands*

As we have seen, Keller "offers a theology of becoming in which the control signified by the *ex nihilo* is given up for the creativity possible from chaos." This has implications for how we understand ourselves, as we have just seen. I further suggest that Keller's tehomic Trinity can encourage in us the virtue of open-endedness. In this section, I first explore two other terms in Keller's work—depth and letting-be—that approximate this virtue, and then I offer, as I have in the previous two chapters, themes in Luce Irigaray's work that help to further define the virtue of open-endedness. In this chapter, I focus on Irigaray's work on the male imaginary and her notion of becoming.

First, themes of depth and letting-be in Keller's work give us some idea of what the virtue of open-endedness is about. The deep of Genesis, according to Keller, is bottomless, resisting closure and opening up the "capacities of an infinite becoming." As we saw earlier, this bottomless depth, or the chaos of creation, has anthropological implications, inviting us to resist easy answers and a preoccupation with orderliness. Keller notes that this kind of "depth" has seldom been thought of as a Christian virtue; "on the contrary, the authorities long ago drained the deep of almost all significance." The virtue of open-endedness, emerging from Keller's tehomic theology, refills the deep.

Likewise, the virtue of open-endedness reflects Keller's concept of "letting-be." She notes that her tehomic Trinity does not order the world into being, as in *ex nihilo* accounts. Rather, God "lets be," in the sense that creation is less an act of power and more an invitation to come into existence; God practices the art of persuasion, not control. The litany of creation in Genesis (let there be light, etc) is more a "whisper of desire" than an imposition of divine control. God's letting-be both is a letting go of absolute control and opens a space for cooperation between God and creation. The person who lets be likewise resists the temptation to impose order or to be in control. The virtue of open-endedness affirms the cooperation, invitation, and interdependency reflected in God's letting-be of creation.

Two themes in Irigaray's work—the subversion of the male imaginary and becoming—also help shape our understanding of the virtue of open-endedness. Irigaray has devoted a good portion of her work to subverting the male economy, or imaginary. By economy, she means the underlying attitudes and assumptions of western culture, which has been male-dominated and tends to eclipse the experiences and perspectives of women. Serene Jones notes four aspects of this male economy: first, it seeks to establish a stable, coherent, and independent subject; second, it erects elaborate conceptual systems in order to "keep ambivalence or ambiguity to a minimum;" third, it makes use of binary opposites of which one term is privileged over the other (e.g., man/woman, culture/nature, etc.); fourth, the central principle (e.g., God) has authority over all other elements of the system because it is self-generated and *a priori*.

This male economy, tied to the morphology of the male body, is concerned with order, linearity, and reason and leads to, as Judith Butler puts it, a "phallogocentrism that claims to be self-constituting." Serene Jones puts it summarily:

Just as the phallus is one, unitary, singular and linear, so too is the dominant Western rationality, which seeks unitary identity and order and which is fundamentally teleological in character. Similarly, just as the phallus needs the hand or another body to know itself, so too Western philosophy assumes that an 'other' is necessary for attaining knowledge and definition of its central principles. This 'other,' however, earns its identity only in so far as it serves the phallus, or in the case of philosophy, in so far as it serves the central, unitary, and stable principle of identity.

In this phallic economy, which privileges sight, the female sexual organ is seen as simply a hole "which has nothing to show for itself." Part of Irigaray's project is to "return to that repressed entity, the female imaginary," which, based female morphology, favors plurality, otherness, and fluidity. "We haven't been taught, nor allowed, to express multiplicity," Irigaray writes, and a return to the female imaginary will open this possibility. The two lips of the female shape make woman always other to herself and upset the rational, linear Oneness of the male imaginary. In a sense, the virtue of open-endedness also aims to subvert this male economy, since it also favors plurality, fluidity, and ambiguity rather than order and control.

Irigaray's work on becoming also give us insights into the virtue of open-endedness. Suggesting that "it is up to humanity to go beyond that which already exists," she argues that humans are in a continual process of becoming. She notes that, in the male economy, human becoming is typically understood as becoming independent or achieving some kind of mastery, whether of the self or of a trade or knowledge. For Irigaray, however, becoming means something more relational. For her, the goal is not mastery or independence, but rather to become "capable of giving and receiving, of being active and passive, of having an intention that stays attuned to interactions, that is, of seeking a new economy of existence or being which is neither that of mastery nor that of slavery." For Irigaray, then, the goal is to "become communicating subjects," to achieve right relations, first, between the sexes, and ultimately among all humans. Further, our own becoming is bound up with the becoming of others: "It is thus a matter of searching for compatibilities between personal becoming and the relation to others. Personal progress cannot be carried out to the detriment of the good of the other...It would be desirable that personal becoming accompany the becoming of the other." Thus, for Irigaray, human becoming is an ongoing process that fosters relationships of respect and equality.

Like Irigaray's understanding of becoming, the virtue of open-endedness is not completely open-ended. Rather, it too directs us to a tentative and somewhat vague *telos;* as with any virtue, practicing the virtue of open-endedness helps us become a certain sort of person, in this case a person who is comfortable with ambiguity and chaos, yet also one who values just and loving relationships. In other words, the virtue of open-endedness is open-ended only in the context of respectful and life-giving relationships. It does not promote a relativistic "anything goes" ethic but one that opens a space for letting go of our need for control, of wanting to define too precisely what it means to be human, of being comfortable with mystery, and participating cooperatively in the movement of all creation towards a peaceful future. Just as Irigaray's "becoming" is a continual process that fosters better relationships, so too is the virtue of open-endedness.

I thus define the virtue of open-endedness, as I have the other two virtues of wonder and self-esteem, in two parts: First, this virtue encourages us to recover and embrace chaos, resisting narratives of self-sufficiency, surety, and control in favor of interdependency, ambiguity, and Keller's "apophatic epistemology of unknowing." Second, in the midst of this chaos, the virtue of open-endedness continues to unfold and affirm differences and to eliminate relationships of domination and abuse, whether between humans or between humans and the earth.

In the beginning of *Face of the Deep,* Keller asks, "What might happen if we ceased to fight, if we let the undertow draw us toward the depths?" The person cultivating the virtue of open-endedness does just this, accepting ambiguity and recognizing her finitude and relative powerlessness in the face of many of life's situations. Open-endedness does not, however, imply passivity, hopelessness, or apathy; this virtue encourages does encourage action—but the action is within chaos, and not against it. As Keller notes, "the trick is to make ourselves at home within uncertainty." Her Trinity engages the chaos, embraces the messiness, and creates something beautiful out of it; the virtue of open-endedness encourages in us the same teho-mophilia—creativity within chaos. As she herself puts it:

Might we live more creatively with the inner and outer chaos—the uncertainty, unpredictability, turbulence, and complexity of our own lives? Our Souls, our sexualities? Or communities? Our cultures? Created in the image of God—can our spirits learn again to vibrate with wisdom on the waters? Perhaps, after all, this is not a mystery to solve but to live with.

Open-Endedness in Action

"The answers are out there in the drowning deep."

-Vienna Teng, "Harbor"

The virtue of open-endedness encourages us to be at home in the messiness and uncertainties of our lives, in our unfinished business, and to see our vulnerabilities and limitations as the very possibility for creativity. As Dorothy Day once noted, we must learn to look on disorder "with a humble serenity, not minding what the neighbors will say." The virtue of open-endedness may also encourage us to let go of our need to categorize people or to define what is human or "normal" too narrowly. Cultivating the virtue of open-endedness might, in Judith Butler's words, allow us to learn "to feel the surety of one's epistemological and ontological anchor go...to learn to live and to embrace the destruction and rearticulation of the human in the name of a more capacious and, finally, less violent world, not knowing in advance what precise form our humanness will take." The virtue of open-endedness, in other words, allows space for our own and others' becoming.

The virtue of open-endedness can apply to issues around sexuality. Below I offer Judith Butler's work as an example of this virtue in action. Running throughout Judith Butler's works are her theory of gender performativity and a concern for sexual minorities. She argues that the binary gender system is oppressive and limiting, and she advocates a different conception of gender that enables all people to be treated with respect and seen as fully human. In her essay, "Performative Acts of Gender Constitution," she addresses individual gender identity, arguing that there is no essential gendered self but rather that the body becomes its gender through a series of acts. For her, gender is a script we are given at birth and asked to perform convincingly. She challenges traditional gender categories, claiming that "there is nothing about a binary gender system that is given." If gender is performative, she argues, and not expressive of an essential, pre-social self, then gender can be reworked and reconstituted. The recognition that gender is performative opens up ways both of subverting essentialized notions of male and female and of opening up more flexible understandings of gender that move beyond the typical binary definition.

It is fairly simple for a person to actively subvert his or her gender; a woman who refuses to wear makeup, for example, or who, in times past, chose to wear pants subverts traditional notions of femininity. Small acts such as these allow individuals to move out of oppressive and essentialized notions of gender, but Butler also proposes a riskier alternative: drag. The work of cross-dressers, and even more so, the existence of transgendered persons, brings about "moments where the binary system of gender is disputed and challenged, where the coherence of the categories are put into question, and where the very social life of gender turns out to be malleable and transformable." Cross-dressers, by subverting traditional notions of gender, highlight in a very obvious way its social construction and challenge us to ask what is real and how things ought to be.

Butler also notes that the binary construction of gender is harmful to anyone who does not fit neatly into the box; this includes effeminate men and "butch" women, in addition to lesbian, gay, transgender, and intersex people. Sometimes, she argues, "a normative conception of gender can undo one's personhood, undermining the capacity to persevere in a livable life." Thus, the overcoming of this conception of gender is a necessary step toward the full flourishing of all humans. She notes the violence that has been done to people who do not conform to the gender norm, which indicates the riskiness of existing outside of those norms. She advocates a nonviolent response that calls for a more capacious understanding of the human, one that can include all people. Such a response will necessarily move away from rigid beliefs about gender and will move into a more open-ended definition, both of gender and of the human person. As she articulates the goal of those outside of the gender box, "we are not simply struggling for rights that attach to my person, but we are struggling *to be conceived as persons.*"

So, Butler seems to offer at least two ways for those oppressed by binary gender constructions to fight that oppression: the first is to act and dress in ways that subvert the dominant gender paradigm, and the second is to work in communities and with organizations to move toward a broader and more flexible interpretation of the human so that violence caused by fear of the "other," or the person who will not fit in a box, will no longer happen. This last point leads Butler to issue a moral guideline: "It may be that what is right and what is good consist in staying open to the tensions that beset the most fundamental categories we require, in knowing unknowingness at the core of what we know, and what we need, and in recognizing the sign of life in what we undergo without certainty about what will come."

Butler's work on sexuality, promoting as it does a letting go of our sureties, a dismantling of violent relationships, and a call for a less rigid sex/gender system, is an example of how the virtue of open-endedness can apply in everyday life. Keller notes that "*to love is to bear with the chaos,*" a project that Butler seems to have embraced. Keller further notes that the church has rarely learned to deal with its own chaos, a fact evident in the way many churches have dealt with the issue of sexuality. The worldwide Anglican church has split over the issue of ordaining gays and lesbians, the Roman Catholic church continues to uphold the unnaturalness of homosexual acts as it reels from a sexual abuse scandal, and, perhaps most disheartening of all, the Pastor Fred Phelps and his Westboro Baptist Church continues to spread his message that "God hates fags." Most Christian churches could use a little practice in the virtue of open-endedness in many areas, including the area of sexuality. Practicing this virtue might enable Christians to see past polarizing debates, to let go of the certainty with which they pronounce their teachings, to revisit their sometimes outdated anthropologies, and to encourage a more positive and welcoming relationship with gay and lesbian Christians. Though many theologians have begun to question traditional views about sexuality, there is still work to be done, and many Christian communities can benefit both from Butler's work on sexuality and the virtue of open-endedness that emerges from Keller's tehomic theology. Many churches still need to learn to bear with the chaos—to love.

Conclusion

"What appears first as formless, a dense shadow shot through with spectral afterimages, may be incubating the form you need. Brood a while longer."

-Catherine Keller, *Face of the Deep*

In this chapter, we have explored the theology of Catherine Keller, examining her use of the four sources and the ways in which her theology affects how we understand ourselves. We saw how Keller engages the process and apophatic traditions, the creation account in the book of Genesis, the experiences of suffering and chaos, the modern sciences, literary theory, and postmodern and feminist theory to offer her own tehomic theology and a Trinity of folds. From this analysis, we saw some anthropological implications of Keller's theology that emphasize relationality and learning to bear with and embrace the chaos within our own lives. We saw how the virtue of open-endedness emerges from Keller's theology to promote greater comfort with ambiguity and a rejection of oppressive relationships. The virtue of open-endedness comes, as the Beatles sing it, speaking words of wisdom: let it be.

6

Applying Trinitarian Virtues

"Theological systems which account for everything and which leave no room for surprise are constricting to the Spirit of God, and are just too neat to be true to reality."

-John Mahoney, *The Making of Moral Theology*

As I have argued throughout this dissertation, our understandings of God are one source of our understandings of ourselves and can shape our ideas of the kinds of people we want to become. In the last chapters, we saw how three particular interpretations of God, drawn from the theologies of John Zizioulas, Elizabeth Johnson, and Catherine Keller, might color our understanding of what it means to be human. John Zizioulas drew heavily from the Christian tradition, particularly the Cappadocian fathers, to offer a trinitarian theology that emphasizes unique and unrepeatable persons and the importance of relationality for that personhood. Elizabeth Johnson drew largely from women's experiences of God to offer a fully feminine image of the Trinity that empowers women to claim their full dignity as human beings. Catherine Keller reexamined the Genesis creation account to offer a Trinity of folds, emphasizing cooperation and interdependence.

From our examinations of these three theologies, it should be clear that different images of God do in fact highlight different aspects of the human and suggest different virtues. We are, however, left with some questions: What now? How do we use multiple images of God and still retain a coherent picture of human life? Which images should we use? How do these trinitarian virtues fit in with other Christian virtues? In this chapter, I begin to address these and other questions. I proceed in three parts: First, I show how the three virtues named in this work—wonder, self-esteem, and open-endedness—can function methodologically, with the help of the four sources, to help determine the most fitting images of God to use. Second, I suggest how these virtues fit in with or modify some of the traditional cardinal virtues (justice, prudence, temperance, fortitude). Finally, I apply all three of these trinitarian virtues to one final case study, in order to show how multiple images of God, virtues, and perspectives can combine to be helpful in making moral decisions.

Wonder, Self-Esteem, and Open-Endedness as Methodological Virtues

THE FOUR SOURCES

In this project, I have examined the trinitarian theologies of John Zizioulas, Elizabeth Johnson, and Catherine Keller, but there are many more theologians and images of God that could be used. How do we decide which images to use? With so many images available, will we be able to have a coherent picture of who God is or who we are? In the first chapter, I addressed these questions somewhat, pointing to the advantages of employing multiple images of God and offering the four sources as one way of helping to determine the fittingness of particular images. In that chapter, I noted the metaphorical nature of our language for God and argued that no metaphor is perfect. Employing multiple metaphors, names, and images for God prevents one image from becoming hegemonic and serves as a reminder that what we are trying to name or describe—God—is ultimately a mystery beyond all naming. I then showed how examining the ways in which a particular theologian engages the four sources can serve as a method for determining the fittingness of their understandings of God. A good image of God will draw from each of the sources, making it consistent with scripture and tradition, while also resonating with contemporary experience and insights from the secular disciplines.

In the three central chapters, I applied this method to show the strengths and weaknesses of three interpretations of the Trinity before I examined their anthropological and ethical implications. From this, we were able to see which sources the theologians employed the most as well as the ones they rarely employed. Zizioulas, for example, drew heavily from tradition, demonstrated a concern that his theology be consistent with his interpretation of scripture, employed philosophy as his main secular discipline and finitude and death as his main experiences. Through this analysis, we uncovered potential weaknesses—an insistence on using the traditional trinitarian formulation (and only that formulation), a potential hierarchy within the Trinity, a lack of real attention to experience—as well as its potential strengths—a deeply traditional account of the Trinity that speaks to contemporary understandings of personhood, an emphasis on uniqueness and unrepeatability, an ontology of communion.

The same method proved helpful in the following two chapters. Johnson began with women's experiences, both good and bad, recovered or reinterpreted aspects of scripture and tradition to be consistent with those experiences, and drew from feminist theory as one of her main secular disciplines. From this analysis, we noted potential weaknesses—a lack of attention to the differences between women, possible misinterpretations of scripture—and strengths—an overdue attention to and affirmation of women's experiences, a creative and deep engagement with scripture and tradition. We saw Keller focus in on one particular aspect of the tradition (the creation account), pay close attention to the scriptural text, draw heavily from modern science, and examine experiences of suffering. From this examination, we noted potential weaknesses—a very non-traditional Trinity, a seemingly haphazard use of philosophers and postmodern theorists—as well as potential strengths—a reinterpretation of the creation account that fits with the findings of modern science and confirms experience, an emphasis on interdependence, a creative and fruitful re-reading of scripture.

The methodological approach of examining a theologian's use of the four sources is thus a useful approach. Such an approach alerts us to the potential shortcomings of a theologian's work, as well as to its strengths. No theologian employs the four sources perfectly, nor does anyone engage each source equally. Some are more thorough and strike a better balance than others; these will tend to be the most fitting theologies to use for ethical projects. Though the work of each of the theologians I examined had its shortcomings, I judge their use of the four sources in their trinitarian theology to be thorough and balanced enough to be fitting.

After I had examined the theologians' engagement with the four sources, uncovering potential strengths and weaknesses, I then explored what each interpretation of God could mean for humans and what kinds of virtues each interpretation might suggest. The practice of these virtues will enable better relationships with ourselves and others. They might also prove helpful in determining which other images of God to use as we bring even more trinitarian theology to bear on Christian virtue ethics. Methodological Virtues

While examining the use of the four sources may be a good enough method to determine the most fitting images of God, some additional criteria might be helpful. The virtues I drew from the three theologians I examined—wonder, self-esteem, and open-endedness—can provide these additional criteria. Thus, the most fitting images of God will not only engage the four sources well but will also in some way practice or promote each of these virtues. It will be helpful to first review the content of each of the virtues, then show how each one can help guide our choice of images of God to use.

First, the virtue of wonder is drawn from Zizioulas' theology. Emphasizing the uniqueness and unrepeatability of each person, both divine and human, he recommends an 'ethical apophaticism' that respects the ultimate unknowability of the other. This idea of 'ethical apophaticism,' combined with insights from Luce Irigaray's work, suggested the virtue of wonder, which I defined in two parts: the first moment of wonder pauses in silent appreciation of the uniqueness of the other and refrains from describing or judging the other, instead allow her to present herself on her own terms. The second moment of wonder consists of analyzing the categories of difference (race, class, gender, etc) that can lead to different kinds of oppression.

Second, the virtue of self-esteem is drawn from Johnson's theology. Turning to women's experiences of oppression and conversion to self-affirmation, Johnson argues that images of God must aid that self-affirmation. She offers She Who Is as a positive, life-giving trinitarian image for women. Drawing from Johnson's theology, along with insights from James Keenan, Paul Wadell, and Luce Irigaray, I offered the virtue of self-esteem. Like wonder, this virtue has two moments: the first moment calls us to affirm ourselves as full human beings as the first step in a broader care for ourselves, and the second moment calls us to challenge social and theological attitudes that exclude certain people from full humanity and make their own self-affirmations difficult to make.

Finally, the virtue of open-endedness is suggested by Keller's theology. Reinterpreting the traditional *creatio ex nihilo* as a *creatio ex profundus*, Keller offers her interpretation of a God of interdependence, enfolding the world and unfolding into it. Keller's Trinity embraces the chaotic depths, favoring creativity and cooperation over sheer power. Keller's theology suggested the virtue of open-endedness, which, like wonder and self-esteem, has two moments. The first moment encourages us to embrace the chaos in our own lives and to resist narratives of self-sufficiency and control. The second moment of open-endedness continues, even within chaos, to affirm differences and to resist patterns of domination and abuse among humans and between humans and the earth.

These virtues help guide different aspects of human relationships and help us grow into the kinds of people we want to become. They can also serve, though, as methodological virtues that can help us choose which images of God we want to uphold as models; in addition to examining the ways in which different interpretations draw from the four sources, we can also use these virtues to give us more precise criteria for the kinds of interpretations of God we want to use. We can extrapolate a principle from each virtue that can help guide any future selection of images of God.

The virtue of wonder yields the following principle: a trinitarian virtue ethics will use images of God that promote respect for uniqueness and diversity. This principle encourages the use of images that draw from the diverse experiences of marginalized people, as well as images that, like Zizioulas', emphasize the uniqueness of the trinitarian persons.

The virtue of self-esteem yields this principle: a trinitarian virtue ethics will employ images of God that encourage the full humanity of every person. This principle encourages the use of trinitarian images that emphasize the equality of the divine persons and that emphasize equality among humans as a central aspect of being created in the image of God. In some ways, the virtue of wonder promotes interpretations of the Trinity that emphasize respect for all the differences among humans, while the virtue of self-esteem promotes interpretations that emphasize the similarities among humans that require us all to be treated equally and that enable us all to love ourselves, regardless of our differences.

Finally, the virtue of open-endedness yields this principle: a trinitarian virtue ethics will employ images of God that do not constrain God or humans to one perspective but rather promote a sense of mystery. This principle encourages the use of trinitarian images drawn in part, like Keller's, from the apophatic tradition that exercise restraint and humility in their descriptions of God. The virtue of open-end-edness also encourages the use of theologies that are attentive to the many scriptural and traditional names and images for God and that enable continued emphasis on the numerous ways of describing the Christian God, and thus, the diverse ways of describing the human person.

All combined, then, we have this as a brief description of the goals of trinitarian virtue ethics: a trinitarian virtue ethics will employ multiple images of God. These images will draw from scripture, tradition, reason, and experience in a thoughtful and balanced way. These images will also promote respect for uniqueness and diversity, encourage the full humanity of every person, and cultivate a sense of the mystery of both God and humans. Reading a theologian through his or her use of the four sources enables us to see areas of strength and of weakness. Using the strengths of a particular image, we can draw out implications for human life and relationships. Noting the weaknesses of a particular image reminds us that no interpretation of God is perfect or complete. The three virtues help ensure that the images we choose encourage wonder, self-esteem, and open-endedness. In addition to giving us insight into the kinds of images of God we would like to use, these virtues can also give us insight into other virtues. In the next section, I explore how our three trinitarian virtues can shape our understanding of the cardinal virtues.

Trinitarian Virtues and Traditional Virtues

The virtues I named are not entirely new; in each of the main chapters I showed how the virtue drawn from the trinitarian theology was similar to virtues or themes in other thinkers' work. I drew from Luce Irigaray's work in each of these chapters in order to define the virtue more precisely. For the virtue of wonder, I drew from Irigaray's own work on wonder and her 'I love to you.' For self-esteem, I drew from Irigaray's work on the divine feminine and subjectivity, as well as from Paul Wadell's work on magnanimity, and James Keenan's work on self-care. For the virtue of open-endedness, I focused on Irigaray's work on fluidity and multiplicity. While the virtues I named parallel themes in Irigaray's work and are strengthened by elements of her work, they can also complement or affect our understanding of some of the traditional Christian virtues. In this section, I briefly show where the virtues of wonder, self-esteem, and open-endedness might fit within a Thomistic account of the virtues.

As we saw in the first chapter, Thomas Aquinas fits the virtues into a natural law framework, so that the virtues help direct us to our natural ends, as well as to our ultimate supernatural end, friendship with God. Thomas, drawing from earlier thinkers such as Aristotle, names prudence, justice, temperance, and fortitude as the cardinal virtues—the virtues upon which all other virtues hinge. Each of the four cardinal virtues has a subset of virtues associated with it. Each of the virtues I named—wonder, self-esteem, and open-endedness—can be associated with at least one of the cardinal virtues.

WONDER

First, the virtue of wonder can be seen as a part of, or perhaps a precondition for, justice. Thomas notes that the proper matter of justice consists of those things that involve our relationships with other people. He defines justice as "a habit by which a man renders each one his due by a constant and perpetual will." Thomas also notes that other virtues can be annexed to justice, as particular aspects of it; "all the virtues that are directed to another person may by reason of this common aspect be annexed to justice." These virtues annexed to justice include religion, piety, observance, and epikeia. Each of these virtues annexed to justice involves relationships with certain people, or in Thomas' terms, giving certain people their due. Religion involves giving due honor to God, and piety involves giving due honor to one's parents and country. Observance involves paying honor to persons in positions of dignity. A person in a position of dignity can include "the governor of a state in civil matters, the commander of an army in matters of warfare, a professor in matters of learning, and so forth."

Finally, the virtue of epikeia involves not giving honor to a particular kind of person but rather knowing when to follow the spirit of the law and not the letter. Because laws are intended to be very general, Thomas argues, they will not be adequate in all situations. Thomas gives the example of a law that requires one to return borrowed goods. In most cases, it will be good and just to return what we have borrowed, but not in all cases. In Thomas' example, it would not be just to return a borrowed sword to a madman because he might injure himself or other people. Thus the virtue of epikeia, which is the subjective part of justice, enables us "to set aside the letter of the law and to follow the dictates of justice and the common good." It makes us aware of the sometimes complex relationship between general laws and particular situations. In some cases, *not* following a law is in fact the best practice of justice and of giving someone his or her due.

Because wonder has to do with our interactions with other people, it is related to justice. It does not, however, guide us only in our relationships with certain kinds of people but with *all* people. I therefore suggest that wonder is not one aspect of justice but rather that it is a precondition for justice. The virtue of wonder disposes us to value the uniqueness of each person, to appreciate the differences between us, and to refrain from imposing our own judgments about a person prematurely. Cultivating an attitude of wonder can thus enable us to act more justly in all of our relationships. Cultivating wonder also cultivates respect for the persons we encounter. Justice without respect is no justice at all; it is "might over right" masquerading as justice. The virtue of wonder, then, renders to all others what is due—respect.

SELF-ESTEEM

Next, we can understand the virtue of self-esteem as a part of fortitude. We have seen already how self-esteem is related to magnanimity; both self-esteem and magnanimity dispose us to strive for greatness. Sometimes, however, it is difficult to strive for greatness, especially under conditions of oppression or discrimination. Thomas himself understood the difficulty of magnanimity, noting that this virtue is "about the hope of something difficult." He thus categorizes magnanimity as an aspect of fortitude because it confirms the mind in hoping for or obtaining the greatest goods.

Self-esteem, which calls for habitual self-affirmation, especially in circumstances that make that affirmation difficult, likewise can be understood as an aspect of fortitude. Whereas magnanimity gives us the courage to believe that we can achieve great goods, self-esteem gives us the courage to believe something more basic—that we ourselves are good. This virtue strengthens us to affirm, even in the most difficult situations, that we are as fully human as the next person.

OPEN-ENDEDNESS

Finally, the virtue of open-endedness can be related to humility (an aspect of temperance) and opposed to the vice of presumption. First, for Thomas, humility is a part of temperance, because it has to do with moderation. Humility, according to Thomas, includes knowledge of one's deficiency and prevents one from aiming at great things against right reason. Though it has often been interpreted negatively, as a quality that encourages unnecessary self-effacement or subservience, the virtue of humility does not in fact encourage such subjugating qualities. Indeed, a humility that is degrading is a false humility; true humility simply encourages a person to know where his or her weaknesses lie. It is the virtue of being honest with one's self. Thomas further argues that "humility makes us honor others and esteem them better than ourselves, insofar as we see some of God's gifts in them." Acquiring the virtue of humility thus enables us to be honest about our own limitations and to appreciate the strengths of others.

In addition to an aspect that encourages us to recognize our limitations and see the good in others, the virtue of humility can also have an epistemic aspect. Practicing the virtue of humility thus encourages us to let go: to acknowledge that we do not have as much control as we think we do, and do not know as much as we think we know. This virtue opens a space for new ideas and perspectives to be heard. The virtue of humility might allow us to learn to acknowledge that our point of view is not the only one and to be willing to deal with complex and confusing issues honestly. In short, the virtue of humility encourages us to be honest about our shortcomings (but not to exaggerate them) and to recognize the strengths of others. The virtue of open-endedness encourages this type of epistemic humility by instilling a sense of mystery. It encourages us to be at home in the unknown, to resist thinking that we have all the answers, and to humbly acknowledge our limitations.

Second, the virtue of open-endedness can be contrasted with the vice of presumption. Thomas notes that it is "vicious and sinful...that any one should assume to do what is above his power: and this is what is meant by presumption, as its very name shows." He further argues that one may be presumptuous in two ways. The first kind of presumption happens "when a man thinks he has greater virtue, or knowledge, or the like, than he has." The second kind happens when "he thinks himself great, and worthy of great things, by reason of something that does not make him so, for instance by reason of riches or goods of fortune." In other words, we fall prey to the vice of presumption when we fool ourselves into thinking that we are better than we actually are, whether by thinking that we have greater virtue or knowledge than we actually do, or by thinking that money or good fortune automatically qualifies us for greatness. The virtue of open-endedness can thus serve as a corrective to the vice of presumption, for the reasons I mentioned above: open-endedness requires honesty with ourselves about what we know, reminding us of our partial and limited perspectives. A sense of mystery, cultivated by the virtue of open-endedness, helps prevent presumption.

TRINITARIAN VIRTUE ETHICS

Incorporating trinitarian theology into virtue ethics does not necessarily introduce major changes into Christian ethics. As we have seen, however, virtues inspired by images of the Trinity can give us new insights into the traditional virtues. The virtue of wonder, drawn from Zizioulas' understanding of the Trinity, gives us new perspectives on justice and helps foster attitudes that make the practice of justice possible. The virtue of self-esteem, drawn from Johnson's trinitarian theology, reminds us that claiming our full humanity often takes a healthy dose of courage. The virtue of open-endedness, inspired by Keller's theology, prevents presumption and fosters epistemic humility by enabling us to feel more comfortable in the chaos of the unknown.

Proposing trinitarian virtues also contributes to the project of incorporating more theology into Christian ethics. As I mentioned in the introduction, over the past decade, Christian virtue theorists such as William Spohn have begun to reflect on the role of Jesus in virtue ethics, and others, such as Joseph Kotva, have explored how the doctrines of sanctification and grace might complement virtue ethics. A handful of thinkers, such as David Cunningham, have also begun exploring the implications of trinitarian theology for virtue ethics. These thinkers have not, however, explored the implications of *multiple* interpretations of the Trinity for Christian virtue ethics.

Employing multiple trinitarian images not only allows us to incorporate more theology into virtue ethics but also allows for many perspectives on both God and humans. Using multiple images of God keeps us on our toes because such an approach leaves room for mystery and new discoveries. Further, employing numerous interpretations of God confirms a central insight of virtue ethics—that life is messy. Many people are faced with morally significant circumstances that are out of their control; lack of good relationships, extreme tragedy, and other factors can influence a person's ability to develop and maintain the virtues, yet these factors are out of the person's hands. The concept of "moral luck" in virtue ethics accounts for these morally relevant contingencies, recognizing that sometimes we are not in total control of our lives or of particular situations.

Virtue ethics, as Joseph Kotva argues, takes a realistic approach to the contingencies and risk in our lives; virtue theory "assumes that we are embodied creatures whose choices and actions are neither completely determined nor completely free." We work out our actions and develop our virtues in the midst of relationships, social circumstances, tragedy, and the general messiness of everyday life. Further, virtue ethics deals with ordinary, everyday actions; nothing is unimportant in the acquisition of virtue. Every voluntary act is considered morally relevant, and a person is encouraged to continually work on all aspects of his or her character; "the *telos* is always before us, always calling us toward a fuller realization of the best life for humans to live." In virtue theory, everything matters.

Kotva also notes that virtue ethics is unable to give a "full-blown, systematic theory of deliberation with precise, math-like, calculations for action." Virtue theory acknowledges the messiness and confusion of human life, and resists a calculative, rational approach to the moral life because it is unrealistic. We work out the virtues as we live and encounter new dilemmas and relationships; virtue ethics can give the basic outline of the moral life, but its content is worked out in real life experience. The virtues of wonder, self-esteem, and open-endedness, along with the many other possible trinitarian virtues, help us to accept the messiness of our lives while also giving us direction for the concrete actions we need to take in order to become compassionate, respectful, and confident human beings. Both virtue ethics as a method and the practice of employing multiple images of God acknowledge the messiness of our lives and help us to deal with it realistically and in creative, life-giving ways.

Using Multiple Images and Applying Multiple Virtues: A Final Case Study

GENERAL APPLICATION

Each of the theologians I examined emphasized, in their own way, the importance of relationships. Zizioulas offered an ontology of communion, in which our relationships constitute our personhood. Johnson emphasized trinitarian relationships of mutuality and equality, which serve as models for human relationships. Keller emphasized the radical relationality of process theology, emphasizing the interdependence within God, between God and creation, among humans, and between humans and the earth.

Luce Irigaray, too, is concerned with relationships. Much of her work has focused on cultivating better relationships, whether the relationships between women and men, the relationships between cultures, or the relationships between humans and the earth. In a public lecture given in June 2010, Irigaray offered her thoughts on how to cultivate better relationships among humans. Drawing widely from much of her work from the last three decades, she enumerated several steps, or ethical gestures, that must be taken in order to cultivate relationships of respect. These gestures begin within oneself and then move outward towards other people. Some of the ethical gestures that Irigaray names correspond to the virtues of wonder, self-esteem, or open-endedness and show us a few concrete ways of putting these virtues into practice. I elaborate below on Irigaray's contributions as a general application of trinitarian virtues. Later, I apply the virtues to a more specific issue.

The first ethical gesture Irigaray names is breathing. Drawing from her own practice of yoga, Irigaray suggests that breathing returns us to ourselves: "We have forgotten that to be cultivated amounts to being able to breathe, not only in order to survive, but in order to constitute a reserve of breath as a soul that helps us to transform our natural life into a spiritual life." The next gesture Irigaray names is dwelling within one's own self-affection. Physical gestures, such as breathing, along with closing the mouth and eyes, enable us to "return home," to cultivate our own identity. For Irigaray, this self-affection means "a capability of peacefully staying within and returning to oneself." Such a return to ourselves cultivates our subjectivity so that we are able to open our own world to welcome the other, Irigaray's third gesture. Meeting and welcoming the other requires going beyond the boundaries of the self to affirm the singularity and freedom of that other. For Irigaray, there is a constant flow between opening oneself to the other and returning back into oneself. The following quotation is lengthy, but it expresses very well this flowing back and forth between our own selves and the other (and it might even express the core of Irigaray's broader ethical project):

Taking the risk to open one's own world in order to meet with another world requires that a return to one's own world be secured. Taking shelter, gathering within oneself is crucial for the one who left one's home to expose oneself to the other, a foreigner or a stranger with regard to oneself. Creating an opening in the horizon of a personal or collective world puts the limits of this world into perspective. Furthermore, crossing the closure of our world deprives us of the environment of known settings, objects and people that we confuse with our irreducible dwelling. The weaving of a familiar world is undone and we feel lost and might ruin our subjectivity and singularity without returning home. We need to go back to the life we were accustomed to in order to, little by little, become capable of building a relation with the other in the respect of our mutual differences.

Irigaray's next gesture is to employ silence as a place of meeting. She suggests that silence is a world of welcome to the other, who has left his or her own world, and indicates our own ability and desire to open ourselves to the unknown. Silence announces to the other that "we preserve a space outside of ourselves and of our world to let the one who is coming arrive," and prepares us for the next step, listening. Listening, for Irigaray, is not simply about transmitting and receiving information but is, rather, about "opening myself to a future that has not yet happened and that I venture to welcome." Listening is about opening ourselves to the world and language of the other, which, although in some ways like our own, is nonetheless different and unique. Then comes the next gesture, speaking in another way, which, like listening, involves more than transmitting information and requires respect for differences. Such a speaking, Irigaray argues, "aims to develop the relations with oneself and with the other rather than to master the world, especially the living world, through words."

The next gestures involve respecting the transcendence of the other, by perceiving the other as a subject rather than an object and contemplating this other "as an irreducible presence whose core will always remain invisible to me." These ethical gestures that Irigaray proposes move toward a deep respect for the mystery of the other. Moving between gestures of self-affection, silence, listening, speaking differently, and recognizing the mystery of the other will enable us to respect the unique world of the other as well as our own.

Further, Irigaray's project of practicing ethical gestures can incorporate each of the three virtues I have named. The gestures of breathing and dwelling within one's self-affection, as well as periodic returns to ourselves after interacting with others, help foster the virtue of self-esteem. Such actions bring us back to ourselves so that we are not swallowed up by our interactions with others. The action of intentional breathing in particular grounds us and allows us to return to ourselves for a moment of self-affirmation. Irigaray's gestures of silence and listening help us to cultivate the virtue of wonder by helping us leave a space between ourselves and the other. These are concrete ways to practice the virtue of wonder. By becoming silent and resisting the impulse to speak, we allow a friendly place of meeting between ourselves and another. By cultivating good listening skills, we show respect for the words, stories, and perspectives of another. Respecting the transcendence of the other and a gradual letting go of our assumptions helps us to practice the virtue of open-endedness. Acknowledging the mystery of another person helps us to become more comfortable with the unknown and prevents us from wanting to judge or categorize people too hastily. Irigaray's ethical gestures offer several concrete ways to put our trinitarian virtues into practice. These gestures can be practiced daily, in our interactions with all the people we encounter. In the next section, I show how these trinitarian virtues can apply in a more specific case.

TRINITARIAN VIRTUES, CHURCHES, AND DISABILITY

I begin with a brief anecdote. I have a friend who became quadriplegic after a football accident about twelve years ago, though I have only known him for about four years. Two years ago, he wanted to take a trip up to Tilden Park in Berkeley because he had never been there. My car could not accommodate him, so he looked up the bus schedule. We hopped on the bus in downtown Berkeley, only to find that the bus into Tilden Park just runs on the weekends. Unfortunately, this was a Tuesday. The bus driver was very friendly and told us where we could get off and walk to the park, so that is what we did. The walk to the park entrance ended up being much longer than we thought, about a mile and a half. There were no sidewalks, so we walked along the side of the road. I was worn out by the time we got there, and the battery for his wheelchair was running low. While we were in the park, he wanted to go around the lake, but the path is not paved and was too uneven for his chair. We settled for sitting by the lake and watching other people walk around it.

We were both worried about how we were going to get home. We found a map in the park and tried to locate a closer bus stop, since he thought his wheelchair might not have made the mile and a half trek back to our original stop. It looked like there was another stop about two-thirds of a mile away, so we headed in that direction. When we got out of the park and back onto the main road (still no sidewalks), we realized that the stop we wanted was straight up; the Berkeley hills can be very steep, and this was one of the steepest. So, without any other options, we headed up, hoping his chair would make it.

After about ten seconds of going up the hill, the engine of his wheelchair overheated, the chair came to a stop and then began rolling backwards. I scrambled to get behind it before my friend rolled all the way down the hill or the chair tipped over. After overheating, wheelchairs take about thirty seconds to cool down before they allow the driver to continue, so we rested, in the middle of the street and only about one-sixth of the way up the hill, while I held on tight to the back of the chair. He assured me the chair would make it the rest of the way, but we were both skeptical. Even though we were both anxious, we were also able to see the humor of the situation—a stalled wheelchair in the middle of the street going up an extremely steep hill must have been quite a sight! Eventually, the engine cooled and he was able to continue. We headed farther up the hill. Ten seconds later, the wheelchair overheated again. I ran to the back of the chair, and we waited another 30 seconds. This happened four more times before we made it to the top of the hill and saw with relief that the bus stop was just a bit further.

I tell this story because it illustrates some of the minor inconveniences a person in a wheelchair faces everyday: lack of reliable public transportation, unpaved paths, and a limited range because of the wheelchair's battery life. I still laugh about this event with my friend, and he faces more serious challenges on a daily basis: narrow doors, lack of space in public restrooms, uneven sidewalks, buildings without ramps or elevators. He has these frustrating experiences in Berkeley and San Francisco, two of the more handicap accessible cities in the United States.

One of the most often overlooked groups of marginalized people is those with disabilities. In addition to hostile or patronizing treatment from many, people with disabilities, especially physical impairments, often have a difficult time just getting around. Things that many people take for granted, such as entering a building with steps, answering the telephone, or using a public restroom, become difficult, or even impossible, tasks for people with physical disabilities. Many of the inconveniences people with disabilities face stem not from their actual disabilities but rather from the ways in which buildings and cities are constructed. It is important to distinguish between a disability, which is a physical impairment in itself, and a handicap, which is an additional impairment placed upon people with disabilities by society.

Churches contribute to the handicapping of disabled persons. The National Organization on Disability notes that, "among the millions of Americans with disabilities, many have spiritual needs that are not being met. They cannot even enter the church, synagogue, meetinghouse, mosque or temple of their choice. Or when they do enter, they may be unable to negotiate stairs or narrow doorways. Some find print too small to read, sound systems that are inadequate, bathrooms they cannot use or an atmosphere that is hostile."

TRINITARIAN VIRTUES AND DISABILITY

How can our virtues—wonder, self-esteem, and open-endedness—help us make our churches welcoming and accessible to everyone? First, the virtue of wonder might enable us simply to notice persons with disabilities at all. In addition to omitting the needs of people with disabilities from our building plans, too often, we as individuals glance down or look away when we encounter someone with a physical disability. John Throop, an Episcopal priest with a vision impairment, notes that "those with full use of their bodies and minds have struggled to welcome differently-abled persons into ministry and leadership—or even to enable them physically to enter into all areas of the church building." We may struggle to welcome people with disabilities into our worship communities because we feel awkward and do not know what to say or how to act. Practicing the virtue of wonder in these situations will enable us to notice a person with disabilities, respect her just as we would any other person, and create a welcoming space—both physically and personally—for both of us to meet.

The virtue of self-esteem might also help in these types of situations; when we feel comfortable and confident in ourselves, it is often easier to interact with other people. The second moment of self-esteem—empowering others—is especially relevant here. Practicing this aspect of self-esteem prompts us to challenge attitudes that run the risk of denying certain people their full humanity. These kinds of attitudes certainly exist about people with disabilities; people with disabilities are made fun of, treated awkwardly or as children, and are denied access to buildings or other public spaces. John Throop gives us a challenge: "every congregation needs to move through some intense self-examination, reflecting on the readiness to welcome fully and completely those who are differently-abled." Churches and good church-going Christians are not immune from having negative attitudes towards people with disabilities. Practicing the virtue of self-esteem requires us to challenge disrespectful types of behaviors and the attitudes (both social and theological) that prompt them, so that the virtue of self-esteem will be a little bit easier for everyone to practice.

Finally, the virtue of open-endedness can help churches and individual Christians offer a better welcome to people with disabilities. This virtue may encourage us to recognize the contingencies we all face and to more fully acknowledge the frailty of all human beings. Keller's theology reminds us that differences are always unfolding. As they unfold, more and more people's voices are heard, and the often unseen ways in which these differences have led to oppression come to light. The virtue of open-endedness challenges us to unfold ability as a site of difference and to make changes, both in our attitudes and in our architecture, that acknowledge and respect differences in ability.

Throop notes that churches can make these types of changes in a three-step process. The first step is to guarantee accessibility; people with disabilities should be just as able to physically enter any space in the church as anyone else. The next step Throop notes is accommodation. This involves offering special classes and services for people with disabilities, such as a special prayer service, having volunteers help with transportation, or having a separate Sunday school class for children with special needs. The third step, after accessibility and accommodation, is acceptance. This step achieves full participation in ministry for all people, including those with disabilities. This final step ensures that people with disabilities are integrated into the community and can actively participate in the life of the church as lectors, choir members, Eucharistic ministers, etc. The move from accommodation to acceptance ensures that people with disabilities are seen as full members of the community and not as "special," peripheral members. The virtue of open-endedness can help us unfold an awareness of disability into our churches and take the steps necessary to guarantee that people with disabilities can become full and active participants in the community.

UNIVERSAL DESIGN

Many organizations, including churches, across the country have already begun to take steps to welcome people with disabilities. One strategy in use is Universal Design, a set of architectural principles that aims to make spaces and appliances usable by everyone, across the range of physical and mental abilities and across the whole human life span. There are seven principles of Universal Design. The first is equitable use, which means that space design should be useful to people with diverse disabilities, and the design should avoid segregating or stigmatizing any users. The second principle is flexibility of use, which means that space and appliances should be designed to accommodate a wide range of individual preferences and abilities. The third principle of Universal Design is to keep design simple and intuitive, making sure the design is easy to understand, regardless of a user's experience, knowledge, language skills, or other factors. The fourth principle is perceptible information, which means that the design should communicate necessary information effectively to the user. This might mean employing different modes of communication (pictorial, verbal, tactile) to present information and to make sure essential information is displayed obviously. The fifth principle of Universal Design is tolerance for error. Design should minimize the hazards of accidental or unintended actions by providing warnings of errors and including fail safe features. A simple example of this is the "undo" button in word processing applications. The sixth principle is low physical effort, which requires that space and appliances can be used comfortably with minimized physical effort. An example of this is push-down door handles (rather than turn knobs) and light, rather than heavy, doors. The final principle of Universal Design is to make sure that size and space is appropriate for use, so that important elements of the design are readily reached or manipulated by any user, regardless of body size, posture, or ability.

The National Catholic Partnership on Disability (NCPD) has offered more particular suggestions for how parishes can incorporates the principles of Universal Design. Some of these suggestions are fairly simple and inexpensive to implement: using large-print missalettes, organizing volunteers to help with transportation or sign-language interpreting, and making sure meetings are held in accessible locations. Other suggestions might be more difficult to implement, depending on the layout of the church, such as providing equal access to the altar/lectern, rectory, reconciliation rooms, and other important spaces. The NCPD also gives more specific suggestions for parishes that are financially able to make renovations: wide doors, modification of bathrooms, installation of elevator, etc. They note that not all parishes have the financial resources to become fully accessible, and they suggest that parishes partner with other nearby parishes, so that between the two, or between a group of four or five, every person can be accommodated. One parish might have sign-language interpreters, for example, while another might have ramps, and still another might have an elevator or Braille hymnbooks.

The NCPD does argue that one project all parishes can undertake, regardless of their economic situations, is to work on changing attitudes towards handicapped people. They note that "the most challenging barriers faced by people with disabilities are the negative attitudes of others, including those which convey stifling pity, fear, or repressive misconceptions about a person's abilities" and suggest having a training session for parish staff and volunteers to familiarize them with the needs and concerns of people with disabilities. The NCPT offers some common sense approaches for interacting with people with disabilities, such as: treat them like you would any other person, feel free to ask about their disability, treat people with disabilities as adults and not like children, respect their personal space, let them do things for themselves, unless they ask for help, etc. Such common sense actions can go a long way in making everyone feel more comfortable, abled and disabled alike.

Working to change attitudes and beginning to incorporate the principles of Universal Design are two concrete ways for churches to offer a better welcome to people with disabilities and to practice the virtues of wonder, self-esteem, and open-endedness. In combination, the exercise of these virtues in the effort to fully integrate people with disabilities into church life will enable Christians to simply notice those with disabilities, to listen to their needs and perspectives, to work to foster an environment in which everyone can practice self-esteem, to make buildings more accessible, and to continue to work to ensure that, in church and in society, *all* people are respected.

Conclusion

The trinitarian virtues I have enumerated in this work—wonder, self-esteem, and open-endedness—can be applied in several ways. In this chapter, I showed how they can be applied as methodological virtues to help determine further trinitarian images to employ, how they can be applied in conversation with the traditional cardinal virtues, and how they can be applied generally from day to day and in the particular instance of churches' treatment of people with disabilities. Each of these virtues gives its own unique insight into these situations, but they are not so disparate as to conflict or become unintelligible when they are employed together. The differences among the virtues of wonder, self-esteem, and open-endedness reflect the different theological perspectives of John Zizioulas, Elizabeth Johnson, and Catherine Keller, respectively. Though each of these theologians offers a point of view that is quite different from the others, they all draw from tradition, scripture, experience, and secular disciplines of knowledge. Each of their theologies is unique, but they all offer recognizable and fitting images of the Christian Trinity. Employing multiple images of God in trinitarian virtue ethics offers us multiple, but not incoherent, perspectives both on God and on the human person. Such an approach preserves a sense of mystery, and, like virtue ethics itself, acknowledges that our lives are messy and that our moral decisions are rarely clear-cut.

Bibliography

Trinity: Keller, Johnson, and Zizioulas

Agora, C. "L'anthropologie théologique de Jean Zizioulas. Un bref aperçu." *Contact* 41:145 (1989): 6-23.

Cumin, Paul. "Looking for Personal Space in the Theology of John Zizioulas." *International Journal of Systematic Theology* 8:4 (Oct 2006): 356-370.

Fox, Patricia. *God as Communion: John Zizioulas, Elizabeth Johnson, and the Retrieval of the Symbol of the Triune God.* Collegeville, MN: The Liturgical Press, 2001.

Fulkerson, Mary McClintock. Review of *She Who Is* by Elizabeth Johnson. *Religious Studies Review* 21:1 (Jan 1995): 19-25.

Groppe, Elizabeth. "Creation *Ex Nihilo* and *Ex Amore*: Ontological Freedom in the Theologies of John Zizioulas and Catherine Mowry Lacuna." *Modern Theology* 21:3 (July 2005): 463-496.

Johnson, Elizabeth. *She Who Is.* New York: Crossroad, 1994.

--------. *Quest for the Living God: mapping frontiers in the theology of God.* New York: Continuum, 2008.

--------. "Author's Response." *Horizons* 31:1 (Spring 2004): 174-186.

--------. *Women, Earth, and Creator Spirit (Madeleva Lecture in Spirituality).* New York, Paulist Press, 1993.

--------. "A Theological Case for God-She: Expanding the Treasury of Metaphor." *Commonweal* (Jan. 29, 1993): 9-14.

---------. "Trinity: To Let the Symbol Sing Again." *Theology Today* 54 no. 3 (1997): 299-311.

Keller, Catherine. *Face of the Deep: A Theology of Becoming.* New York: Routledge, 2003.

--------. *From a Broken Web: Separation, Sexism, and Self.* Boston: Beacon Press, 1986.

--------. *On The Mystery.* Minneapolis: Fortress Press, 2008.

--------. "The Lost Chaos of Creation." *Living Pulpit* 9:2 (April 2000): 4-5.

---------. "Burning Tongues: A Feminist Trinitarian Epistemology." In *Introduction to Christian Theology: Contemporary North American Perspectives,* ed. Roger Badham, Louisville: Westminster John Knox, 1998.

--------. "Seeking and Sucking: on relation and essence in feminist theology." In *Horizons in Feminist Theology,* ed. Rebecca Chopp, Minneapolis: Fortress Press, 1997.

--------. "The Apophasis of Gender: A Fourfold Unsaying of Feminist Theology." *Journal of the American Academy of Religion.* 76:4 (Dec 2008): 905-933.

--------. *Apocalypse Now and Then: A Feminist Guide to the End of the World.* Boston: Beacon Press, 1996.

McFague, Sallie. Review of *Face of the Deep* by Catherine Keller. *Interpretation* 59 (Jan 2005): 82-84.

Papanikolaou, Aristotle. *Being With God: Trinity, Apophaticism, and Divine-Human Communion.* Notre Dame, IN: University of Notre Dame Press, 2006.

--------. "Is John Zizioulas an Existentialist in Disguise? Response to Lucian Turcescu." *Modern Theology* 20:4 (Oct 2004): 601-608.

Russell, Edward. "Reconsidering Relational Anthropology: A Critical Assessment of John Zizioulas's Theological Anthropology." *International Journal of Systematic Theology* 5:2 (July 2003): 168-186.

Schneider, Laurel. Review of *Face of the Deep* by Catherine Keller. *The Journal of Religion* 84:4 (Oct 2004): 639-640.

Schroeder, Paul. "Suffering Towards Personhood: John Zizioulas and Fyodor Dostoevsky in Conversation on Freedom and the Human Person." *St. Vladimir's Theological Quarterly* 45:3 (2001): 243-264.

Schwöbel, Christoph et al. *Persons, Divine, and Human: King's College Essays in Theological Anthropology.* Edinburgh: T & T Clark, 1991.

Turcescu, Lucian. "'Person' vs. 'Individual', and Other Modern Misreadings of Gregory of Nyssa." *Modern Theology* 18:4 (Oct 2002): 527-539.

Walker, Corey. Review of *Face of the Deep* by Catherine Keller. *Journal of the American Academy of Religion* 75:3 (Spring 2007): 733-736.

Zagano, Phyllis and Terrence Tilley, eds. *Things New and Old: Essays on the Theology of Elizabeth A. Johnson.* New York: Crossroad, 1999.

Zizioulas, John. *Communion and Otherness.* New York: T&T Clark, 2006.

-------. *Being as Communion: Studies in Personhood and the Church.* Crestwood, NY: St. Vladimir's Seminary Press, 1985.

-------. "Human Capacity and Incapacity." *Scottish Journal of Theology* 28:5 (1975): 401-447.

-------. "On Being a Person: Towards an Ontology of Personhood." In *Persons Divine and Human: King's College Essay in Theological Anthropology,"* ed. Christoph Schwobel and Colin Gunton. London: T&T Clark, 1996.

Trinitarian Ethics and Other Trinitarian Theology

Althaus-Reid, Marcella. *The Queer God.* New York: Routledge, 2003.

Baker-Fletcher, Karen. *Dancing with God: The Trinity from a Womanist Perspective.* St. Louis: Chalice Press, 2006.

--------. *Sisters of Dust, Sisters of Spirit: womanist wordings on God and creation.* Minneapolis: Fortress Press, 1998.

Bauerschmidt, Frederick. "The Trinity." In *Gathered for the Journey: Moral Theology in*

Catholic Perspective, ed. David McCarthy and Therese Lysaught, Grand Rapids, MI: William B. Eerdmans, 2007.

Cunningham, David. *These Three are One: The Practice of Trinitarian Theology*. Malden, MA: Blackwell Publishers, 1998.

--------. "Participation as a Trinitarian Virtue: Challenging the Current 'Relational'

Consensus." *Toronto Journal of Theology* 14:1 (Spring 1998): 7-25.

Daly, Mary. *Beyond God the Father*. Boston: Beacon Press, 1973.

Danaher, William J. *The Trinitarian Ethics of Jonathan Edwards*. Louisville, KY: Westminster John Knox Press, 2004.

Duck, Ruth. *Gender and the Name of God: The Trinitarian Baptismal Formula*. New York: Pilgrim Press, 1991.

Finger, Thomas N. *Self, Earth & Society: Alienation & Trinitarian Transformation*. Downers Grove, IL: Intervarsity Press, 1997.

The Forgotten Trinity: Volume 1. Report of the British Council of Churches Study Commission on Trinitarian Doctrine Today. London: British Council of Churches, 1989.

Gebara, Ivone. *Longing for Running Water: Ecofeminism and Liberation*. Minneapolis:

Fortress Press, 1999.

Grenz, Stanley. *Rediscovering the Triune God: The Trinity in Contemporary Theology*.

Minneapolis: Fortress Press, 2004.

Gunton, Colin. "The church as a school of virtue? human formation in trinitarian framework." In *Faithfulness and Fortitude: conversations with the theological ethics of Stanley Hauerwas*, ed. Mark Thiessen Nation and Samuel Wells, Edinburgh: T & T Clark, 2000.

-------. *Father, Son, and Holy Spirit: Toward a Fully Trinitarian Theology*. New York: T & T Clark, 2003.

Hunt, Anne. *The Trinity: Nexus of the Mysteries of Christian Faith*. Maryknoll, NY: Orbis Books, 2005.

Jones, L. Gregory. *Transformed Judgment: Toward a Trinitarian Account of the Moral Life*. Notre Dame, IN: University of Notre Dame Press, 1990.

Kärkkäinen, Veli-Matti. *The Trinity: Global Perspectives*. Louisville, KY: Westminster John Knox Press, 2007.

Kimel, Alvin, ed. *This Is My Name Forever: The Trinity and Gender Language for God*. Downer's Grove, IL: InterVarsity Press, 2001.

LaCugna, Catherine. *God for Us: The Trinity in Christian Life*. San Francisco: Harper Collins, 1991.

---------. "God in Communion with Us." In *Freeing Theology*, ed. Catherine LaCugna, San Francisco: Harper Collins, 1993.

McFadyen, Alistair I. *The Call to Personhood: A Christian Theory of the Individual in Social Relationships*. New York: Cambridge University Press, 1990.

McFague, Sallie. "The Ethic of God as Mother, Lover and Friend." In *Feminist Theology: A Reader*, ed. Ann Loades, Louisville, KY: Westminster John Knox, 1990.

Navone, John J. *Self-Giving and Sharing: The Trinity and Human Fulfillment*. Collegeville, MN: Liturgical Press, 1989.

O'Collins, Gerald. *The Tripersonal God: Understanding and Interpreting the Trinity*. Mahwah, NJ: Paulist Press, 1999.

Ramshaw, Gail. *God Beyond Gender: Feminist Christian God-Language*. Minneapolis: Augsburg Fortress, 1995.

Rahner, Karl. *The Trinity*. trans. Joseph Donceel. New York: Crossroad, 1970.

Reinders, Hans. *Receiving the Gift of Friendship: Profound Disability, Theological Anthropology, and Ethics*. Grand Rapids: William B. Eerdmans, 2008.

Ruether, Rosemary Radford. *Sexism and God-Talk: Toward a Feminist Theology*. Boston: Beacon Press, 1983.

Rusch, William, ed. *The Trinitarian Controversy*. Philadelphia: Fortress Press, 1980.

Smail, Thomas Allan. *Like Father, Like Son: The Trinity Imaged in our Humanity*. Grand Rapids: Eerdmans, 2006.

Suchocki, Marjorie. *God Christ Church*. New York: Crossroad, 1989.

-------. "The Unmale God: Reconsidering the Trinity." *Quarterly Review* (Spring 1983): 34-49.

Tanner, Kathryn. *Jesus, Humanity, and the Trinity: A Brief Systematic Theology*. Minneapolis: Fortress Press, 2001.

Tennis, Diane. *Is God the Only Reliable Father?* Philadelphia: Westminster Press, 1985.

Torrance, Alan. *Persons in Communion: An Essay on Trinitarian Description and Human Participation*. London: T&T Clark, 1996.

------- and Michael Banner. *The Doctrine of God and Theological Ethics*. New York: T & T Clark, 2006.

Vanhoozer, Kevin J., ed. *The Trinity in a Pluralistic Age: Theological Essays on Culture and Religion*. Grand Rapids: Eerdmans, 1996.

Volf, Miroslav. *After Our Likeness: The Church as the Image of the Trinity*. Grand Rapids, MI: William B. Eerdmans, 1998.

Webb, Stephen. *The Gifting God: A Trinitarian Ethics of Excess*. Oxford: Oxford University Press, 1996.

Wilson-Kastner, Patricia and Ruth Duck. *Praising God: The Trinity in Christian Worship*. Louisville, KY: Westminster John Knox Press, 1999.

Virtue Ethics

Aquinas, Thomas. *Summa Theologica*. trans. Fathers of the English Dominican Province. New York: Benziger, 1947. http://www.ccel.org/a/aquinas/summa/FP.html.

Cates, Diana Fritz. *Choosing to Feel: Virtue, Friendship and Compassion for Friends*. Notre Dame: University of Notre Dame Press, 1997.

Doris, John. *Lack of Character: Personality and Moral Behavior*. Cambridge: Cambridge University Press, 2002.

Flanagan, Kieran and Peter Jupp, eds. *Virtue Ethics and Sociology: Issues of Modernity and Religion*. New York: Palgrave, 2001.

Gula, Richard. *The Call to Holiness: Embracing a Fully Christian Life.* New York: Paulist Press, 2003.

Gustafson, James. *Can Ethics Be Christian?* Chicago: University of Chicago Press, 1975.

Hauerwas, Stanley and Charles Pinches. *Christians Among the Virtues: Theological Conversations with Ancient and Modern Ethics.* Notre Dame, Ind.: University of Notre Dame Press, 1997.

Keenan, James. "Virtue Ethics." In *Christian Ethics: An Introduction,* ed. Bernard Hoose, Collegeville, MN: The Liturgical Press, 1998.

--------. "Proposing Cardinal Virtues." *Theological Studies.* 56 (1995): 709-724.

--------. "Virtue and Identity." In *Creating Identity,* ed. Hermann Haring, Maureen Junker-Kenny and Dietmar Mieth. London: SCM Press, 2000.

--------. *Commandments of Compassion.* Franklin, WI: Sheed & Ward, 1999.

-------- and Daniel Harrington. *Jesus and Virtue Ethics: Building Bridges between New Testament Studies and Moral Theology.* Oxford: Sheed and Ward, 2002.

Kotva, Joseph Jr., *The Christian Case for Virtue Ethics.* Washington, DC: Georgetown University Press, 1996.

MacIntyre, Alasdair, *After Virtue: A Study in Moral Theory.* 3d ed. Notre Dame: University of Notre Dame Press, 2007.

Murphy, Nancy, Brad Kallenberg and Mark Thiessen Nation, ed. *Virtues and Practices in the Christian Tradition.* Notre Dame, IN: University of Notre Dame Press, 1997.

Porter, Jean. *The Recovery of Virtue: The Relevance of Aquinas for Christian Ethics.* Louisville, KY: Westminster/John Knox Press, 1990.

-------. *Nature as Reason: A Thomistic Theory of the Natural Law.* Grand Rapids, MI: William B. Eerdmans, 2005.

Spohn, William. "The Return of Virtue Ethics." *Theological Studies* 53 (1992): 60-75.

--------. *Go and Do Likewise: Jesus and Ethics*. New York: Continuum Publishing Group, 2000.

--------. *What Are They Saying about Scripture and Ethics?* New York: Paulist Press, 1995.

Stassen, Glen and David Gushee. *Kingdom Ethics: Following Jesus in Contemporary Context*. Downers Grove, IL: InterVarsity Press, 2003.

Tessman, Lisa. *Burdened Virtues: Virtue Ethics for Liberatory Struggles*. New York: Oxford University Press, 2005.

Traina, Cristina L.H. *Feminist Ethics and Natural Law: The End of the Anathemas*. Moral Traditions and Moral Arguments. Washington, D.C.: Georgetown University Press, 1999,

Wadell, Paul. *Happiness and the Christian Moral Life*. New York: Sheed & Ward, 2008.

--------. *The Primacy of Love: An Introduction to the ethics of Thomas Aquinas*. New York: Paulist Press, 1992.

--------. *Becoming Friends: Worship, justice and the practice of Christian friendship*. Grand

Rapids, MI: Brazos Press, 2002.

--------. *Friendship and the Moral Life*. Notre Dame, IN: University of Notre Dame Press, 1989.

Irigaray

Bacon, Hannah. "What's Right with the Trinity? Thinking the Trinity in Relation to Irigaray's Notions of Self-Love and Wonder." *Feminist Theology* 15:2 (Jan. 2007): 220:235.

Bostic, Heidi. "Luce Irigaray and Love." *Cultural Studies* 16:5 (Sept. 2002): 603-610.

Butler, Judith. "Bodies That Matter." In *Engaging with Irigaray*, ed. Carolyn Burke, Naomi Schor, and Margaret Whitford. New York: Columbia University Press, 1994.

Deutscher, Penelope. *A Politics of Impossible Difference: The Later Works of Luce Irigaray*. Ithaca, NY: Cornell University Press, 2002.

Grosz, Elizabeth. "The Hetero and the Homo: The Sexual Ethics of Luce Irigaray." In *Engaging with Irigaray,*. ed. Carolyn Burke, Naomi

Schor, and Margaret Whitford. New York: Columbia University Press, 1994.

--------. "Irigaray and the Divine." In *Transfigurations: Theology and the French Feminists*, ed. Maggie Kim, Susan St. Ville, and Susan Simonaitis. Minneapolis: Fortress Press, 1993.

Irigaray, Luce. "Ethical Gestures Towards the Other." Lecture delivered at University of Nottingham, June 23, 2010.

--------. "Toward a Divine in the Feminine." In *Women and the Divine: Touching Transcendence*, ed. Gillian Howie and J'annine Jobling. New York: Palgrace Macmillan, 2009.

--------. "Introduction." In *Religion in French Feminist Thought: Critical Perspectives*, ed. Morny Joy, Kathleen O'Grady, and Judith L. Poxon. New York: Routledge, 2003.

--------. "Equal to Whom?" In *The Postmodern God: A Theological Reader*, ed. Graham Ward, trans. Robert Mazzola. Oxford: Blackwell Publishers, 1997.

--------. *Sexes and Genealogies*, trans. Gillian Gill. New York: Columbia University Press, 1993.

-------. *This Sex Which Is Not One*, trans. Catherine Porter. Ithaca, NY: Cornell University Press, 1977.

-------. *Thinking the Difference: For a Peaceful Revolution.* trans. Karin Montin. New York: Routledge, 1994.

-------. *An Ethics of Sexual Difference*, trans. Carolyn Burke and Gillian Gill. Ithaca, NY: Cornell University Press, 1984

-------. *I love to you: sketch of a possible felicity in history.* trans. Alison Martin. New York: Routledge, 1996.

-------. *je, tu, nous: Toward a Culture of Difference* trans. Alison Martin. New York: Routledge, 1993.

-------. *Speculum de l'autre femme.* Editions de Minuit, 1974.

Jones, Serene. "This God Which is Not One." In *Transfigurations: Theology and the French Feminists*, ed. Maggie Kim, Susan St. Valle, and Susan Simonaitis. Minneapolis: Fortress Press, 1993.

Joy, Morny. *Divine Love: Luce Irigaray, Women, Gender, and Religion.* Manchester: Manchester University Press, 2007.

-------. "La question de Dieu dans l'oeuvre de Luce Irigaray." *Religiologiques* 21 (2000): 49-60.

Mulder, Anne-Claire. *Divine Flesh, Embodied Word: Incarnation as a Hermeneutical Key to a Feminist Theologian's Reading of Luce Irigaray's Work.* Amsterdam: Amsterdam University Press, 2006.

Rivera, Mayra. *The Touch of Transcendence: A Postcolonial Theology of God.* Louisville: Westminster John Knox, 2007.

Schor, Naomi. "This Essentialism Which is Not One." In *Engaging With Irigaray.* New York: Columbia University Press, 1994

Jones, Serene. "This God Which is Not One." In *Transfigurations: Theology and the French Feminists,* ed. Maggie Kim, Susan St. Ville, and Susan Simonaitis. Minneapolis: Fortress Press, 1993.

Miscellaneous Material

Baier, Annette. *Moral Prejudices: Essays on Ethics.* Cambridge, MA: Harvard University Press, 1995.

Benatar, David. *Better Never to Have Been: The Harm of Coming into Existence.* Oxford: Clarendon Press, 2006.

Burns, J. Patout. *Theological Anthropology (Sources of Early Christian Thought).* Philadelphia: Fortress Press, 1981.

Butler, Judith. *Giving an Account of Oneself.* New York: Fordham University Press, 2005.

--------. *Undoing Gender.* New York: Routledge, 2004.

--------. "Performative Acts and Gender Constitution: An Essay in Phenomenology and Feminist Theory." In *Writing on the Body: Female Embodiment and Feminist Theory,* ed. Katie Conboy, Nadia Medina, and Sarah Stanbury. New York: Columbia University Press, 1997.

Cady, Duane. *Moral Vision: How Everyday Life Shapes Ethical Thinking.* New York: Rohman and Littlefield, 2005.

Cahill, Lisa Sowle. *Sex, Gender, and Christian Ethics.* Cambridge University Press, 1996.

The Center for Universal Design (1997). "The Principles of Universal Design, Version 2.0." Raleigh, NC: North Carolina State University.

Clack, Beverly. "Feminism and Human Mortality" in *Feminist Philosophy of Religion: Critical Readings,* ed. Pamela Sue Anderson and Beverly Clack. London: Routledge, 2004.

--------. "Revisioning Death: A Thealogical Approach to the 'Evils' of Mortality." *Feminist Theology* 22 (Sept 1999): 66-77.

Corbett, Sarah. "A Prom Divided." *The New York Times,* May 21, 2009.

Curran, Charles. *The Catholic Moral Tradition Today: A Synthesis.* Washington, DC:
Georgetown University Press, 1999.

Daly, Mary. *Webster's First New Intergalactic Wickedary of the English Language.* Boston: Beacon Press, 1987.

Day, Dorothy. *On Pilgrimage.* Grand Rapids, MI: William B. Eerdmans, 1999; reprint, Catholic Worker Books, 1948.

De Beauvoir, Simone. *The Ethics of Ambiguity.* New York: Kensington, 1948.

DesCamp, Mary Therese and Eve Sweetser. "Metaphors for God: Why and How Do Our Choices Matter for Humans? The Application of Contemporary Cognitive Linguistics Research to the Debate on God and Metaphor." *Pastoral Psychology* 53:3 (Jan 2005): 207-238.

Farley, Margaret. *Just Love: A Framework for Christian Sexual Ethics.* New York: Continuum, 2006.

--------. "The Role of Experience in Moral Discernment." In *Christian Ethics,* ed. Lisa Sowell Cahill. Cleveland: Pilgrim Press, 1996.

--------. "Love, Justice, and Discernment: An Interview with Margaret Farley." *Second Opinion* 17:2 (Oct 1991): 80-91.

--------. *Personal Commitments: Beginning, Keeping, Changing.* San Francisco: Harper and Row, 1986.

--------. "Feminist Consciousness and the Interpretation of Scripture." In *Feminist Interpretation of the Bible*, ed. Letty Russell. Philadelphia: The Westminster Press, 1985.

--------. "Sources of Inequality in the History of Christian Thought." *The Journal of Religion* 56 (April 1976): 162-176.

--------. "New Patterns of Relationship: Beginnings of a Moral Revolution." *Theological Studies* 36 (Dec. 1975): 627-646.

Friedman, Marilyn. *What are Friends For? Feminist Perspectives on Personal Relationships and Moral Theory.* Ithaca, NY: Cornell University Press, 1993.

Garreau, Joel. *Radical Evolution: The Promise and Peril of Enhancing Our Minds, Our Bodies—and What It Means to Be Human.* New York: Broadway Books, 2005.

Goffman, Erving. *The Presentation of the Self in Everyday Life.* New York: Anchor Books, 1959.

Guroian, Vigen. *Incarnate Love: Essays in Orthodox Ethics.* Notre Dame, IN: University of Notre Dame Press, 2002.

Gustafson, James. "The Place of Scripture in Christian Ethics: A Methodological Study." In *Readings in Moral Theology #4: The Use of Scripture in Moral Theology,* ed. Charles Curran and Richard McCormick. Ramsey, NJ: Paulist Press, 1984.

Henold, Mary. *Catholic and Feminist: The Surprising History of the American Catholic Feminist Movement.* Chapel Hill: Univ. of North Carolina Press, 2008.

Hochschild, Arlie. *The Managed Heart.* Berkeley: Univ. of California Press, 2003.

Hodgson, Peter and Robert King, ed. *Christian Theology: An Introduction to Its Traditions and Tasks.* Minneapolis: Fortress Press, 1994.

Johnson, Elizabeth, ed. *The Church Women Want: Catholic Women in Dialogue.* New York: Crossroad, 2002.

Johnson, Mark. *Moral Imagination: Implications of Cognitive Science for Ethics.* Chicago: University of Chicago Press, 1994

Jones, Serene. "Women's Experience Between a Rock and a Hard Place: Feminist, Womanist, and Mujerista Theologies in North America." In *Horizons in Feminist Theology* ed. Rebecca S. Chopp and Sheila Greeve Davany. Minneapolis: Fortress Press, 1997.

Kant, Immanuel. *Foundations of the Metaphysics of Morals*, 2nd ed., trans. Lewis White Beck. Upper Saddle River, NJ: Prentice Hall, 1997.

Keenan, James. "Fundamental Moral Theology: Tradition." *Theological Studies* 70 (2009): 140-158.

Lakoff, George. "The Contemporary Theory of Metaphor." In *Metaphor and Thought.* Ed. Andrew Ortony. (Cambridge, England: Cambridge University Press, 1993). P. 202-251

Lederach, John Paul. *The Moral Imagination: The Art and Soul of Building Peace.* Oxford University Press, 2005.

Martin-Alcoff, Linda. "The Problem of Speaking for Others." *Cultural Critique* (Winter 1991-2): 5-32.

Matsuda, Mara. "Legal Theory Out of Coalition." In *Feminist Theory Reader: Local and Global Perspectives,* 2nd ed., ed. Carole McCann and Seung-kyung Kim. New York: Routledge, 2010.

McDougall, Joy Ann. "Keeping Feminist Faith with Christian Traditions: A Look at Feminist Christian Theology Today." *Modern Theology* 21:1 (Jan 2008): 103-124.

McFague, Sallie. *Metaphorical Theology: Models of God in Religious Language.* Philadelphia: Fortress Press, 1982.

Melville, Herman. *Moby Dick,* Norton Critical Edition. New York: W.W. Norton & Co., 2002.

National Catholic Partnership on Disability. "Creating an Access Plan Using the Principles of Universal Desgin. www.npcd.org/accessible-design/universal.

National Organization on Disability (2005), *That All May Worship: An Interfaith Welcome to People with Disabilities.*

Ryan, Maura and Brian Linnane, S.J., ed. *A Just and True Love: Feminism at the Frontiers of Theological Ethics: Essays in Honor of Margaret Farley.* Notre Dame, IN: Notre Dame Press, 2007.

Saint-Exupéry, Antoine de. *The Little Prince,* trans. Katherine Woods. New York: Harcourt, Brace, and World Inc., 1943.

Schüssler Fiorenza, Elizabeth. *But She Said: Feminist Practices of Biblical Interpretation.* Boston: Beacon Press, 1992.

Schwöbel, Christoph et al. *Persons, Divine, and Human: King's College Essays in Theological Anthropology.* Edinburgh: T & T Clark, 1991.

Throop, John. "Total Ministries and Persons with Disabilities." *Clergy Journal* 85:5 (May/June 2009): 9-11.

Walker, Margaret. *Moral Understandings: A Feminist Study in Ethics.* New York: Routledge, 1998.

Weaver, Mary Jo. *Springs of Water in a Dry Land: Spiritual Survival for Catholic Women Today.* Boston: Beacon Press, 1993.

www.ingramcontent.com/pod-product-compliance
Lightning Source LLC
Chambersburg PA
CBHW060513130626
46553CB00002B/480